DATE DUE

BRODART   Cat. No. 23-221

MR ROCKEFELLER'S R·O·A·D·S

The Untold Story of Acadia's Carriage Roads & Their Creator

BY

ANN ROCKEFELLER ROBERTS

DOWN EAST BOOKS

*In memory of my grandfather,
from whom I learned many things,
and who has become my friend.*

Book design by Janet Patterson
Color separations by Four Colour Imports
Printed and bound at Courier Stoughton, Stoughton, Mass.

5 4 3 2 1

Down East Books
P.O. Box 679
Camden, ME 04843

Contents

Acknowledgments

The most important resource used for this book has been the extensive archival material at the Rockefeller Archive Center in Tarrytown, New York. Their large collection of personal and business letters, newspaper clippings, maps, and other materials has been invaluable in reconstructing the sequence of events and the opinions and attitudes of JDR Jr. and others. In addition, the National Park Service archives in Washington, D.C., Boston, and Mount Desert Island revealed important information about the roles of park officials and some of the correspondence of George Dorr, the first park superintendent. A number of books and articles on Mount Desert Island provided background materials and shed light upon the history of this part of the Northeast. *John D. Rockefeller, Jr., A Portrait*, Raymond Fosdick's definitive biography, was invaluable in giving an understanding of the forces that shaped JDR Jr. and in describing his personality. *John D. Rockefeller: The Cleveland Years*, by Grace Goulder, gives a full and sympathetic description of John D. Rockefeller, Sr., as a private person and of his early years in Cleveland. Among various books and articles on Mount Desert Island itself, *The Story of Mount Desert Island*, by Samuel Eliot Morison, and *Mt. Desert Island and Acadia National Park: An Informal History*, by Sargent F. Collier, were the most helpful. George B. Dorr's own narrative, *The Story of Acadia National Park*, is wonderfully colorful, full of anecdotes, as well as informative. Will Rieley's excellent study of the carriage roads, commissioned by Acadia National Park and completed in May 1989, was an important addition to my research. Finally, a series of personal interviews with people who knew JDR Jr., or were involved with some phase of the Acadia National Park carriage-road project, were most helpful in giving a more personal sense of the man and yielded some of the more revealing stories about him.

No book such as this would have been possible without the cooperation of many knowledgeable people, and I am most grateful for the time and attention that have been generously given by so many. Will Rieley gave me the initial encouragement to undertake the independent study that in time led me to write this book. During the period when my dissertation was being prepared, we shared the material we each found at the Rockefeller family archives. Subsequently he and Roxanne Rouse completed the definitive technical study of the Acadia National Park carriage roads for the National Park Service, a work of scholarship that I would recommend to any professional in our field. Reuben Rainey was a wonderfully wise and patient adviser while I was at UVA, giving unstintingly of his time and attention. He always spotted the weaknesses in the text and never failed to urge me on to excellence. The staff at the Rockefeller Archive Center in Tarrytown was most courteous and always ready to assist in finding materials. Dr. Joseph Ernst, the emeritus director and founder of the archives, shared most generously his considerable archival knowledge and his personal recollections of JDR Jr. Dr. Darwin Stapleton (the director), Tom Rosenbaum, and Melissa Smith were especially attentive to and patient with my innumerable requests for letters and photographs. Marie Callahan cheerfully produced a mountain of photocopies. The National Park Service personnel, whether in Maine, Washington, or Boston, constantly impressed me with their devotion to park issues and their affection for Acadia. They always gave thoughtful assistance. My thanks go particularly to Isabel Mancinelli, Lois Winter, and Curt Mossestad at the Acadia National Park office on Mount Desert Island. Robert Pyle of the Northeast Harbor Library, Gladys O'Neil of the Bar Harbor Historical Society, and Deborah Burch of the Seal Harbor Library gave me invaluable leads and contacts as well as access to the materials in their archives.

My special thanks also go to the many people who shared their time and personal recollections of JDR Jr. and the building of the carriage roads. These include Ray Wylock, the former superintendent to JDR Jr. at Pocantico Hills, New York; Irene Hill Marinke of Bar Harbor, Maine, the daughter of engineer Walters G. Hill; and Charles and Peggy Simpson of Seal Harbor, Maine. The Simpsons put at my disposal not only their time and memories but also the extensive personal collection of letters and photographs Charles inherited from his father and grandfather—all of which has added greatly to the book. Within my own family, I am particularly indebted to my uncles Laurance and David Rockefeller, and to my mother, Mary C. Rockefeller, for sharing their personal recollections of JDR Jr. in Maine. My daughter, Mary Louise Pierson, shared her photographic skills and contributed most of the color pictures of the roads and bridges.

Many people worked diligently with me on the research and in the preparation of the manuscript, and without their collective skills and good judgment, I would have been hard put to come to a conclusion. Christina O'Leary-Rose, Michael Keating, Jackie Wong, and Tracey Carroll all helped to uncover important pieces of the story or pertinent photographs from diverse sources. Tim Roybal, Tina Surman, and Stuart Rosenthal lent their expertise to the preparation of the final manuscript. My editor at Down East Books, Karin Womer, was wonderfully supportive and patient with my struggles as a new author, skillfully shepherding the book to completion. David Outerbridge made keen comments on the original manuscript and lent his assistance to finding a publisher. Kathy Brandes did a superior job of editing the final text. Kathy Garrett worked unstintingly with me on the maps so that the final product contains original work of a high quality. Ann O'Neill assisted in the final preparation of the photographs. Finally, my special thanks go to my husband, T George Harris, for his sharp editorial eye, his loving support, and his patience with long nights, irregular schedules, and irregular humors.

Introduction

Anyone who visits Acadia National Park sooner or later encounters the carriage roads. It is impossible to hike in the eastern part of the park without crossing these graceful byways meandering through the landscape. As a child and young woman summering with my family on Mount Desert Island, Maine, I was, of course, aware of their presence. I hiked along and across these roads with my friends every summer as we explored the inner reaches of Acadia National Park. But like most children, I just took them for granted—like the hiking trails, they seemed to my child's perception to have been there always—and it never occurred to me to investigate their source. As time passed, I gradually became aware that they somehow were related to my grandfather's beneficence, as was so much else that I encountered. However, my grandfather, John D. Rockefeller, Jr., was an extraordinarily modest and private man, and he rarely discussed with his grandchildren any of the work he was doing. This reticence was characteristic of the rest of my family as well, so my knowledge remained vague and incomplete.

Years later, in my third year of a master's program in landscape architecture, I began looking for an independent project that would have meaning to me as both a student of design and a conservationist. As I searched, it became increasingly clear that there were fascinating garden designs right in my own family's backyard, so to speak. Wherever he lived, Grandfather's houses had been set in beautiful gardens, and at first it appeared that I could do a fine study of one of these gardens. However, one of the gardens had already been written about in some detail, and the more closely I looked at the others, the more intrigued I became with his personal role as opposed to that of the designers. It became apparent that he did not just commission someone to submit a design; he was intimately involved with every stage of the work—from the concept to the most minute details of execution. He showed all the symptoms of having been a designer himself.

At this point, through coincidence and good fortune, one of my professors offered me the chance to do some research on the Acadia National Park carriage roads, and I decided to find out what Grandfather's role had been there. As I looked at the publications on the carriage roads and studied the history of Mount Desert Island, there was confusion about who was responsible for the concept and design of the roads. Some authors attributed the design to Frederick Law Olmsted without designating which one, Senior or Junior, and others attributed the roads to one of the architects who designed the bridges. No one in any of the publications I saw even considered that Grandfather might have actually laid out the roads himself. Apparently they found it hard to imagine that someone of his wealth would have the necessary skills or would want to do the work. But as I delved deeper into the family archives, it was soon apparent, to my delight and fascination, that here Grandfather had been the sole designer as well as the patron. Frederick Law Olmsted, Sr., died long before the roads were conceived, and his son Frederick, Jr., although known by my grandfather, was not involved in the project until the 1930s, after most of the roads were built (see Appendix E). I no longer had any doubt about what subject to choose for my dissertation.

Between 1913 and 1940, a period of twenty-seven years, my grandfather designed and constructed fifty-seven miles of carriage roads on Mount Desert Island, Maine, as part of his effort to offer the public a way to experience nature. He was also involved in the creation of Acadia National Park, hoping that this park would be, as he put it, "a real gem of the first water among national parks." Many of these carriage roads were built on his own private land that he later donated to the government; others were built on government land, or land owned by a private conservation organization. No other carriage-road system of comparable quality and extent exists in the national park system. Acadia's roads are also unique because their construction is exemplary, because they are essentially the work of one man, and because they are reserved to this day for pedestrians, horse riders, and carriages. Automobiles are banned from them.

To learn how and why these roads were built, I began to study the thinking and the habits of my grandfather. His prescience fills the history of the carriage roads, from concept and design to the details of each bridge and carriage turnaround. The roads, an expression of his vision for Acadia National Park, arose from his deep personal feelings for the earth and its beauty, his conviction that the Divine Presence is revealed in nature, and his belief that nature plays an important role in our lives. I found him to be a diligent, self-denying man who worked very hard at many tasks and would have felt guilty about an evening during which he did not labor at some worthy service. Even in shifting a road stake a few yards to give horseback riders a better view of the mountains above, he was driven by a seriousness and dedication to service that characterized his life.

The carriage roads were not built without controversy, however, and as I listened to my mother talking about her recollections of early summers on Mount Desert and of her own parents, I suddenly realized that within the two branches of my immediate family were the two sides of the controversy that wound like a thread through the history of the carriage roads. My maternal grandfather, Percy H. Clark, represented the opposition. In the early 1900s, he had come to Northeast Harbor with his family seeking a summer retreat, and he bought a wonderful rambling cottage on the shore. It was the first house designed and built by noted architect Welles Bosworth after he graduated from the Ecole des Beaux-Arts in Paris. This same architect would later design and build bridges on the Acadia carriage roads for my grandfather Rockefeller.

Grandfather Clark, a devoted outdoorsman, spent many hours in the mountains and on the waters of Mount Desert. He was an accomplished canoeist, and my mother described how he fearlessly paddled the ocean in his canoe as the Indians had before him, going out into the Western Way and to the outer islands. Once he paddled the entire perimeter of Mount Desert Island in two days, stopping along the shore at night to camp with his companion. He took his children on long walks into the mountains and valleys, showing them the hidden springs of pure water and instructing them about the flora and fauna. He was a close friend of George W. Pepper, one of the major opponents of the carriage roads, and the two of them laid out many of the footpaths in the mountains on the western side of Mount Desert.

So when the "Rockefeller Roads" (as they were locally dubbed) began to spread toward Northeast Harbor, Grandfather Clark did not take kindly to them. He told his children in no uncertain terms that they were a grave mistake and a desecration of the wilderness. Mother was brought up to think that John D. Rockefeller, Jr., was a misguided man indeed, and a "spoiler of the wild." When a carriage road was cut out across the side of Cedar Swamp Mountain and left a conspicuous scar visible from the main road leading to Northeast Harbor, Mother and her friends would point it out as they drove by, as evidence of the horrible destruction being wrought. However, Grandfather Clark was never part of the active opposition to the roads, and his distaste for them did not seem to impede the progress of my parents' courtship—or the cordial relations of the two families after their marriage. Years later, after the Great Fire that raged across the Island in 1947, my two grandmothers carried on a very warm correspondence on the subject. Grandmother Clark not only sent her sympathies for the destruction to the park but also expressed her great concern over the damage to Grandfather Rockefeller's carriage roads.

The struggle at Acadia reflected a deep division in approach to conservation, one that persists to this day. The carriage roads opened up the inner regions of the island's center in ways that deeply upset many early summer residents. Their view that the wild should remain pristine was shared by such notable early conservationists as John Muir and John Burroughs, both of whom gained many supporters through their writings. JDR Jr.'s view—that the benefits of the wild should be preserved but made available and enhanced by humans—was shared by men such as Gifford Pinchot, first director of the National Forest Service, and Horace Albright, third director of the National Park Service. A strong case can be made for either point of view. At Acadia, JDR Jr.'s view predominated because he had the power and the perseverance to pursue it.

One can also argue that, given the location of Acadia National Park within easy access of much of the Eastern Seaboard and the heavy use it receives today (more than four million visitors a year), the carriage roads actually protect the park's wild lands. The roads provide access to the interior in a controlled, planned way, so visitors can explore remote portions of the park without destroying it. They also allow maintenance workers to tend the park without having to cut or bulldoze temporary access roads for their equipment. The terrible fire of 1947 proved how important the roads could be in an emergency, and fifty years after their construction they are still used and cherished by numerous park visitors.

The automobile represents another of the wonderful ironies of both my family and the carriage roads. Its introduction onto the island was one of the principal reasons that Grandfather began to build the carriage roads. At the same time, the automobile's immediate and extraordinary success was the cause of the stupendous growth of the Standard Oil Company and its subsidiaries after the turn of the century, from which came all the Rockefeller wealth. Without the car, the family fortune that allowed Grandfather to help create Acadia National Park and build the carriage roads would not have existed, and yet Grandfather's roads were built in order to keep the car at bay.

The carriage roads were constructed during the first part of the twentieth century, when major technological and social changes were underway in America—changes that had been gathering momentum since the final settlement of the West in the late 1800s. Extensive railroad networks to service industrial, agricultural, and population growth were rapidly being built. Commercial electric lighting, the telephone, and farm machinery were all moving in. The United States was shifting from being a predominantly agricultural nation to an urban one, and in the process was becoming an economic giant and a world power. This rapid development lent itself to the rise of aggressive entrepreneurs such as my great-grandfather, John D. Rockefeller, Sr., and his contemporaries.

My grandfather grew up amid all this change, watching the agricultural ideal give way before the industrial maelstrom. The Jeffersonian dream of each family's members living and supporting themselves on their own land was replaced by the philosophy of industrialization. By 1920, the country was for the first time more urban than rural; many people worked indoors in factories instead of out in the fields. They traveled in trains or cars at rates of speed that insulated them from the sounds and smells of the earth. The car—the invention that provided the greatest mobility for the largest number of people—became a major factor between 1919 and 1929. By then, most Americans lived in houses that protected them from the vagaries of the weather but also removed them from nature's cycles and rhythms. Remarkable and welcomed labor-saving devices such as the electric washing machine and dryer, indoor plumbing, and running water increasingly kept everyone inside and separated from the earth. In fact, nearly every invention born of modern technology served to insulate people more and more from the land.

At the same time that all this development was taking place, there came the first glimmerings of new attitudes toward the wilderness—attitudes that ultimately resulted in the birth of our national park system and the conservation movement. In 1890, the frontier was officially closed, indicating that Americans felt they had effectively conquered the wilderness and her native peoples and that there was no longer unlimited land to be usurped by settlers. As settlements became more secure and the European population more firmly entrenched, these new Americans no longer saw themselves only as aggressive conquerors, fearful settlers, or ambitious exploiters of natural resources. Some even began to look to the wilderness as something positive; others longed for its imagined freedoms and charms. And with these changed attitudes came a newfound desire to preserve it.

By 1872, Yellowstone had become the first national park, following the establishment of Yosemite Valley as a state park in California in 1864. John Muir was crusading for the preservation of our forests and mountains, and writers such as Henry David Thoreau, John Burroughs, and James Fenimore Cooper were extolling the American landscape in new ways. As a schoolboy and college student, Grandfather absorbed some of this literature reflecting the shifting attitudes toward the frontier and the wilderness, and it profoundly affected his later life.

To JDR Jr., road building was much more than a passion indulged in for its own sake. It was a consumate skill used in service of a larger mission: to unfold for the public the wonders of nature in Acadia National Park and to offer the chance to reestablish bonds with the earth. His devoted friend and former head of the National Park Service, Horace Albright, wrote about JDR Jr.'s feelings in his journal:

> I am often asked why did he expend so much for the magnificent roads, trails, culverts—everything so perfectly thought out, the best money could buy? Well, he expressed his thoughts on this many times, in many places and concerning many different areas—not just Acadia. It could be summed up in a word—FITNESS! His philosophy was somewhat like that of the Chinese with their balanced ying-yang or again with the Navajo belief of harmony or walking in beauty. Humans need a quiet, peaceful atmosphere, a conformation with nature. A road that cuts straight through a forest is not in harmony with nature, for a deer or bear does not create a straight path. Man-made bridges of concrete, steel or brick upset the balance of beauty in a natural surrounding, but the rocks of the creek bed do not. And so on and so on. I believe Mr. Rockefeller had a genuine distaste for the garish advances of civilization—and what's more he feared them. So he took every opportunity he felt possible to step in and save his fellow humans from the onslaught of the crippling effects of an industrial society.[1]

JDR Jr. had no intention of imposing a personal style or making a personal statement as a designer. Rather, he made every decision in service of the larger purpose. His point was to arrange the elements to reveal beauty, not to make a beautiful arrangement. It was not necessary for him to design the sites; they were already there, the handiwork of God waiting to be seen by humans. He was creating pathways by which the users of the land would be able to see it, to feel part of it, and thereby be restored.

To complete this monumental task, JDR Jr. needed the full breadth of the technical skills he had honed over the years as road builder, the acuity of his designer's eye, and all of his considerable knowledge of the terrain. His absorption in each step of the process and his constant insistence on making careful on-site decisions becomes entirely understandable; he had to study the particular circumstances of each place and to adjust the roads as they were being built so that they would fulfill their purpose in every detail. The grade of each segment, the degree of curvature, and the line of the road had to carry viewers so smoothly from one spot to another that they would not be aware of the transitions. The elements, bridges, gate houses, culverts, and the roadbeds themselves are appropriate to their particular function, each designed for its place. The reforestation and extensive roadside plantings not only calmed and delighted the eye; they were designed to let the roads blend back into the landscape. Above all, it was the landscape that counted.

As a result of this philosophy, the design of the roads is masterful, and their construction shows the highest level of craftsmanship. The roads themselves are almost invisible; they blend into the land as if they had always been there.

The carriage roads allow us to move out of civilization and into the woods in a safe and contained manner now that the fearsome wilderness described in early accounts of Mount Desert has been made secure and inviting. They enable us to renew our connection with nature, a connection that offers both physical and spiritual solace. If civilization at its best is what makes us whole, and if one element of being whole is being in concert with our environment, then the carriage roads at Acadia National Park are indeed a civilizing piece of work.

CHAPTER 1

The Making of A Landscape Artist

The philanthropic work of John D. Rockefeller, Jr., is well known and covers an astonishingly broad spectrum, in terms of both subject matter and geography. His interests included education, health, medical research, historic restoration, the temperance movement, labor issues, and conservation. The projects he funded were located in areas that spanned the breadth of this country and beyond. France, Greece, Israel, China, and Japan were among the other countries that benefited from his generosity. But his work on the land—the one element about which he cared most deeply, and to which he committed his personal creative energies—is little known.

The carriage roads he built at Acadia National Park on Mount Desert Island in Maine are the chief expression of this hidden passion.

John D. Rockefeller, Jr., was born on January 29, 1874, at 997 Euclid Avenue, Cleveland, Ohio. The fifth child and only son of John D. Rockefeller, Sr., and his wife, Laura Spelman Rockefeller, he was eagerly welcomed by his parents. He was destined to be not only the sole male heir but also the devoted companion of his father in leisure pursuits as well as in business and philanthropy.

At the time of young John's birth, his father was already a man of considerable wealth and renown. The Standard Oil Company, of which he was the founder, had been incorporated for nearly two years and was expanding rapidly. This success allowed the senior Rockefeller to situate his growing family in a manner that not only indicated his means but, more important, reflected his tastes in landscape and leisure.

Several years before young John's birth, his father had purchased property on Cleveland's fashionable Euclid Avenue. On the lot stood a handsome, if ponderous, house surrounded by luxuriant lawns and gardens. JDR Sr. added a stone and pine-paneled stable for his thoroughbred trotters that rivaled the house for splendor. Later he purchased an adjacent lot so he could extend his gardens and

Opposite: **John D. Rockefeller, Jr., in his thirties, at the time he was building the carriage roads.** *Seal Harbor Historical Society*

9

FIG. 1.—JOHN D. ROCKEFELLER'S PAIR—MIDNIGHT, RECORD 2.18¼, AND FLASH, RECORD 2.19¼.

John D. Rockefeller, Sr., driving a favorite matched pair, Midnight and Flash. *National Trust for Historic Preservation*

plant more trees. His father, William Rockefeller, had always selected farms with an eye toward the beauty of the land, and he had never been without fine horses. JDR Sr. inherited his father's eye for natural beauty and learned from him the pleasure and value of thoroughbreds, as well as the fine art of riding and driving. So, in turn, young John was surrounded by gardens, trees, and the finest horses as far back as he could remember.

The unusually clear values and ideals of the family into which JDR Jr. was born were an important foundation for his life's work. Whatever motives drove his father to build an oil monopoly and become one of the richest men in the country, the beliefs handed down to JDR Jr. demanded that no matter how this only son chose to direct his energies, it should include the greater good of the community.

JDR Jr.'s parents were devout Baptists whose religious beliefs pervaded their daily lives. Their religious practice included morning and evening prayers as well as Sunday school and Sunday church services. Their social life revolved around church suppers, visits with clergy, and church friends. They taught their children the importance of duty, self-discipline, personal responsibility, and social commitment. Wealth was never seen as a reason to abandon Christian ideals or become self-indulgent. It was to be used wisely, without waste, and for the good of society. The children were taught to keep careful accounts of their expenditures and to tithe at a very early age. Next to the church, the family was regarded as the central, sacred, and most important institution, and theirs was a singularly close-knit and caring group. As JDR Jr.'s biographer, Raymond Fosdick, wrote, "Home and church were not just the dominating influences, they were the only ones."[1]

Years later, in an address JDR Jr. made for the fiftieth anniversary of a men's Bible class that he taught, he described in some detail the family's home religious life. The modesty he had learned as a Christian precept impelled him to tell the story entirely in the third person:

> In their home, family prayers before breakfast had always been the custom, each one taking part, either reading from the Bible in turn or reciting a verse of scripture, many of which were thus learned and vividly retained throughout life. The blessing was asked before each meal. On Sunday the parents and children went together to church and Sunday school. The father was superintendent of the school, the mother superintendent of the primary department, the children as they grew older often acted as supply teachers. Friday night was prayer meeting night; the whole family always attended the meeting. At an early age the children were encouraged by their mother to take part like the older people, either in a brief prayer or a word of personal experience.
>
> Sunday was invariably observed as a day of rest, only necessary duties were performed. A cold dinner was the rule, that work might be reduced to a minimum. No studying was allowed or games of any kind; the reading of the Bible and Sunday books only, was permitted. If the children had done wrong during the week, their mother would point out to them earnestly how in so doing they had sinned against God whose forgiveness she would lead them to seek in prayer. The day was a happy day, for it was a family day.[2]

It also seems to have been understood that JDR Jr. was to follow in his father's footsteps in some way. There was never any question of his finding a separate career; he was to carry on his father's work, and he was trained and prepared for this role from the time of his birth.

In contrast to the seriousness of this pious and regulated home life was their outdoor summer life at Forest Hill on the outskirts of Cleveland, a property JDR Sr. purchased shortly after the birth of his son. In 1878, when John was four, the family began spending summers there, a practice that lasted for thirty-five years. The landscape

"Across this sloping hillside of carefully maintained lawn, Mr. Rockefeller enjoyed from his residence this magnificent view over the woodlands to the shores of Lake Erie." From A.D. Taylor's Forest Hill Park, 1938. Rockefeller Archive Center

was enough to delight any child. There were hills, ravines, two lakes, streams, and woodlands for exploring. It was "a wonderland, a vast green province providing happy freedom to offset their otherwise circumscribed routine . . . they did much of their growing up in this land that lay as nature had made it."[3] A page from Fosdick's conversations with JDR Jr. conveys wonderfully well the deep pleasure the Rockefeller children must have had at Forest Hill. Fosdick noted that JDR Jr. "said there was a beech tree at Forest Hill over a creek and each of the children had a seat in it—a limb carved with his or her own name. They used to sit there a great deal and someone would read aloud. During this time they knitted or crocheted or did fancy work and Jr. carved road signs out of wood for the roads of Forest Hill." It was here that JDR Jr. learned from his father to love the outdoors. It was here that he learned the skills of road layout and landscaping that led to his extraordinary work at Acadia National Park.

Forest Hill "reawakened [JDR Sr.'s] boyhood love of the out-of-doors," Grace Goulder observed, adding that "[it] brought to the surface . . . a latent but very real talent for landscaping."[4] The senior Rockefeller gradually expanded the property until it encompassed more than seven hundred acres of rolling countryside—an enclave apart from his increasingly public working world yet within driving distance of his offices in downtown Cleveland. And as JDR Sr. gradually developed his country estate, his growing son often accompanied him while he worked. The entire family became very attached to the Forest Hill retreat, as it held a large part of their familial history, and fond memories of growing up, family gatherings, and summer outings. So even after they had moved to New York and begun to establish a new country home along the Hudson River, they faithfully maintained and returned to Forest Hill until JDR Jr.'s mother died in 1915. In 1917, the house burned down.

Years later, when the Forest Hill estate was being given to the city of Cleveland for a park, the care with which it had been laid out was evident to A.D. Taylor, the prominent landscape architect involved with its redesign for public use. In his proposal to the city in 1938, he wrote, "In addition to the preservation of the existing natural features, trees and shrubs of a great variety were planted, lawn areas were developed and maintained, and miles of winding gravel roads, bridle trails and foot paths were constructed on the upper area in the vicinity of the residence, and through the deep and attractive ravines on either side of the residence plateau."[5]

Taylor understood the involvement of both father and son: "Mr. Rockefeller also laid out a half-mile track for exercising his fast driving horses. . . . On either side of this drive, JDR Jr., as a boy, planted a row of maples which today provide fine shade for that portion of the track. . . ."[6] It is easy to imagine the young John working earnestly under his father's encouragement, planting the little maple seedlings that would grow to maturity as the child did, becoming a more and more important part of his father's world.

In addition, JDR Sr. built two lakes at Forest Hill by damming streams that ran through the property. He saw to it that one was large enough for boating, swimming, and skating—some of his favorite activities with his children. To carry his carriage roads and footpaths across the ravines and over the streams, he installed rustic little bridges made of native stone procured from a quarry on the premises. Existing clumps of fine specimen trees captured his interest, and he became proficient in their cultivation and manage-

Forest Hill Park, 1938.
Young JDR Jr. planted this
row of maples along the
half-mile driving track.
Rockefeller Archive Center

ment. He also developed his own nursery for both trees and shrubbery for landscaping. There were stables for his horses and a fully functioning farm that produced ample provisions for his family, as well as houses for estate employees and their families.

At the time JDR Sr. was working on Forest Hill, other wealthy families were also developing large estates along the Eastern Seaboard. The major influence on the design of these estates was a book entitled *A Treatise on the Theory and Practice of Landscape Gardening Adapted to North America*, first published in 1841 by a horticulturist from the Hudson River Valley named Andrew Jackson Downing. His ideas were an exposition of what he described as the "Modern, Natural, or Irregular Style" derived from the informal English land-

This pleasure drive across an earthen dam beside one of the artificial lakes at Forest Hill shows JDR Sr.'s skills of road layout and landscaping. JDR Jr. would make similar use of coping stones on the Mount Desert Island carriage roads. From A.D. Taylor's *Forest Hill Park, 1938. Rockefeller Archive Center*

At Forest Hill, rustic bridges of stone quarried on the property were built along the network of carriage roads and paths. *Rockefeller Archive Center*

scape types popular at the time, and he described landscape gardening as "an artistical combination of the beautiful in nature and art
. . . a union of natural expression and harmonious cultivation, capable of affording us the highest and most intelligent enjoyment to
be found in any cares or pleasures belonging to the soil." As Downing
saw it, man and nature collaborated in two basic forms of expression
for this Natural Style: the beautiful and the picturesque. The beautiful landscape came from the use of simple flowing shapes both for
the plantings and the architectural elements of a site to produce "a
fullness and softness of outline and perfectly luxuriant development." Trees of "graceful habit and flowing line" were favored, such
as the elm and the chestnut. The beautiful was also attained by "the
removal or concealment of everything uncouth and discordant, and
by the introduction and preservation of forms pleasing in their
expression."

In contrast, the picturesque landscape consisted of "striking,
irregular and spirited forms" grouped in "a negligent manner" for a
wilder feeling. Larch and pine trees were considered appropriate for
this. Downing intended that both variations be governed by the
principles of unity and variety to achieve "the production of a whole
and the proper connexion of the parts." Downing described one
Hudson River estate in language that makes it sound nearly identical
to Forest Hill: ". . . the native woods and beautifully undulating
surface, are preserved in their original state, the pleasure grounds,
roads, walks, drives and new plantations, have been laid out in such
a judicious manner as to heighten the charms of nature. . . . The park
. . . afforded a delightful drive within itself, as the whole estate
numbered about 700 acres."[7]

The winding shores of the lakes at Forest Hill, the curving
roads, and the generous tree plantings are so much in harmony with
Downing's precepts that it seems quite possible that JDR Sr. drew
ideas from the most popular landscape design source of his day. This
atmosphere permeated young John's consciousness as he grew as
well, and there are indications both in his later correspondence and
in the design of the carriage roads that these concepts influenced his
thinking.

Forest Hill was a private and self-sufficient retreat, a place
where JDR Sr. found the freedom to relax with his family and teach
his children the outdoor activities he especially enjoyed. He gave
them ponies at an early age, and soon all four were accomplished
riders. In looking for a mount for young John, JDR Sr. wrote to a horse
dealer: "I want a very gentle one of that size for a little boy of seven
years of age. Something lazy and surely safe."[8]

JDR Jr. with his pony,
about 1884. *Rockefeller
Archive Center*

To JDR Jr., as a young boy, his father was a beloved companion,
teacher, and friend. The importance of their relationship is clearly
stated in his own recollections of their times together:

From the days of our childhood, Father was always a companion and
friend to his children. . . . He was patient and encouraging as a swimming
teacher and resourceful in devising mechanical means of helping us to
learn to swim. In my mind is a picture of him swimming around the lake,
a distance of nearly a mile, on a hot summer day with his straw hat on to
keep his head cool.

He also taught us to row and was an enthusiastic skater. In the yard on
each side of 4 West 54th Street, the New York home, Father had cement
floors laid with curved edges, so that they could be flooded with water,
thus making a skating rink. Here for a number of years we skated during
the winter days, and many neighbors and friends enjoyed the sport with
us. . . . I can see him now, with his hat on, doing the "outer edge" for a few
moments in the morning before leaving for his office. Well do I recall how
one winter when I was staying at Forest Hill and Father was there on a
visit, his enthusiasm for skating led him to get up shortly after midnight
on a Monday morning to go with some of the workmen to our little lake
to see about having the surface of the ice flooded so as to make it
smoother for skating the next day. He would not have the work done on
Sunday.

I also recall going with Father once to test the thickness of the ice on
the lake to see if it was safe for skating. The lake was deep, so we took
under each arm long narrow boards, which would hold us up in case we
broke through the ice. That was characteristic of Father. He always took

the utmost care to examine any project thoroughly; then when convinced that it was safe, put it through without further question. . . .

One of the pleasures of our childhood days at Forest Hill was walking through the woods with Father on little paths which he enjoyed laying out. I remember also long drives with him out into the surrounding country behind his fast horses. . . .

Another sport which we enjoyed together was bicycling, of which Father was very fond. Moonlight nights we often went riding with Father through the woods in both roads and paths. The one riding ahead would tie a handkerchief to the back of his coat and then ride the most difficult course he could find, thus testing the skill of the others in making their way through the winding paths. When the leader, as often happened, would be led off the path or road to follow the wake of the bright moonlight, resulting eventually in the overthrow of the entire party, our delight reached its height.[9]

As John matured, he was encouraged to participate in the workings of Forest Hill in other ways that developed his skills and his knowledge of people. He derived great pleasure from cutting and splitting wood, for instance, and spent one January learning the art of maple sugaring. When he reached the age of sixteen, he was put in charge of the payroll for the estate workers and began to oversee the various landscape and construction projects then underway.

In spending time with his father, and participating as Forest Hill was being developed, John learned the fine points of laying out a road: how to follow the contours of the land and lay a grade that would easily accommodate a carriage, how to seek the best views, and how to design a sequence of experiences that would reveal the best features of the land. Surrounded by the beauty of the natural world, he was being trained to recognize the best criteria for the harmonious landscaping of nature—and then was encouraged to appreciate it by a father who already did.

JDR Sr. himself described his passion for road design and his interest in aligning the road with the best views:

How many miles of roads I have laid out in my time I can hardly compute, but I have often kept at it until I was exhausted. While surveying roads, I have run the lines until darkness made it impossible to see the little stakes and flags. . . . This planning for good views must have been an early passion with me. I remember when I was hardly more than a boy I wanted to cut away a big tree which I thought interfered with the view from the windows of the dining room of our home.[10]

Speaking of their later home at Pocantico Hills, JDR Sr. wrote:

At Pocantico Hills, New York, where I have spent portions of my time for many years in an old house where the fine views invite the soul and

Father and son bicycling at Forest Hill in the 1880s.
Rockefeller Archive Center

where we can live simply and quietly, I have spent many delightful hours studying the beautiful views, the trees and fine landscape effects of that very interesting section of the Hudson River.

. . . I had the advantage of knowing every foot of the land, all the old big trees were personal friends of mine, and with the views at any given point I was perfectly familiar—I had studied them hundreds of times. . . . In a few days I had worked out a plan so devised that the roads caught just the best views at just the angles where in driving up the hill you came upon impressive outlooks and the ending was the final burst of river, hill, cloud, and great sweep in country to crown the whole; and here I fixed my stakes to show where I suggested the roads should run, and finally the exact place where the house should be.[11]

JDR Jr.'s long childhood summers of relative freedom allowed him to wander at will through meadows and woods, and they imbued him with a deep love of nature that he carried throughout his life. For him, not only was the natural world full of beauty, but its beauties were a gift that showed the hand of the Creator. Years later, he would

The Forest Hill roads were carefully laid out to follow, not challenge, the land's contours, a principle JDR Jr. was later to follow when planning Mount Desert's carriage roads. *Rockefeller Archive Center*

often refer to this belief in many of the speeches he was called upon to deliver.

As I watched barren winter give way to the sudden onrush of spring in a Virginia garden a few months ago, I marveled as never before at the miracle of nature's rebirth. Where the garden borders were one day a lifeless expanse of dull earth, almost overnight they had become a riot of color, form and design. There were countless pansies, no two of whose friendly faces were alike. Tulips of endless variety and hue, gay little primrose, daffodils that looked like molten gold in the sunlight, not to mention the many other flowers that went to make up the magic carpet spread out in the garden. When I looked at the trees and saw millions of tiny buds one day, on twigs that seemed only dead the day before, while almost overnight I found myself sitting under the grateful shade of their green leaves; when I saw the grass put on the refreshing green of its new growth almost as suddenly as the setting [sun] suffuses with a delicate pink the fleecy white clouds that have hurried into the sky to bid it good night; when I realized what infinite organization and planning were involved in the coming of spring in just one garden and tried to fancy what the multiplication of that event in nature's worldwide realm meant, I said to myself: How can anyone who has witnessed the miracle of the spring doubt the existence of an eternal creative force in the world, call it nature, or God, or what you will?[12]

The strong religious feelings of JDR Jr.'s parents and the love of natural beauty that he shared with his father and his paternal grandfather certainly laid the foundations for his belief in nature as evidence of a Creator. It seemed obvious to him that if God was in all things human, He surely was manifest also in the natural world He had created.

JDR Jr. was also familiar with contemporary literature that expressed similar views. Among his favorites were Washington Irving's *The Sketch Book of Geoffrey Crayon, Gent.*, James Fenimore Cooper's novels, and Ralph Waldo Emerson's essays. In fact, he carried his school copy of Irving's *Sketch Book* with him for many years. As he said at the opening celebration for the renovated Sunnyside, home of Washington Irving in Tarrytown, New York, "The little volume I hold in my hand is the copy of Washington Irving's *Sketch Book* which I used in school nearly sixty years ago. In it are many passages marked on the margin, then or in later life, because of their beauty and meaning."[13]

For both JDR Sr. and his son, the design of a beautiful landscape went hand in hand with the means to be part of it. To them this meant riding and driving as well as walking, and their concept of how a place should be laid out was shaped by these activities. The roads were to be ample for a carriage to pass through comfortably, the paths wide enough for horses as well as pedestrians. Views and vistas were planned for the height of a rider or carriage passenger as well as for those on foot. Underlying all of these thoughts was the fundamental one that it was "good" and "pleasurable" to be involved in nature in this way. Beauty was not found exclusively in the wild and primitive part of nature; it could also be found in a nature loved and tended by man. The "beautiful" had to do with "order" and "neatness," and nature could be experienced as a sequence of "views" of scenery "improved" by human intervention. This philosophy underlay the basic design JDR Jr. later developed into a unique road system at Acadia National Park.

The standards of quality advocated by JDR Sr. were very high. As with his business enterprises, he used meticulous planning and scrupulous attention to detail on every project at Forest Hill. (There is a story told about JDR Sr.'s early days at the Standard Oil Company in which it is said that, in order to have the greatest possible economy, he figured out exactly how many nails were necessary to secure the top of a full barrel of oil. He determined that exactly nine

Coaching in Central Park was a fashionable pastime around the turn of the century, and the Rockefellers were often to be seen there.
New York Historical Society

nails would do—fewer than the standard number used in the trade—and he calculated how much money that would save the company.) Part of this concern for detail extended to his interest in the well-being and working environment of the people in his employ. He inspired loyalty in those who worked for him, and there were employees who stayed for many years. JDR Jr. was to emulate these traits and adopt them in his own work. As biographer Raymond Fosdick reported, JDR Jr. acquired "a taste for perfection and a passion for taking pains."[14] These characteristics were to manifest themselves decades later in the highest quality of work on every detail of Acadia's granite-based carriage roads.

In 1875, a year after JDR Jr.'s birth, JDR Sr. began taking his family to New York City for the winters, since his business increasingly called for him to be there. And as the children grew older, rides in Central Park supplemented those on their own roads at Forest Hill. JDR Sr. was regarded, as his son wrote, "as one of the best gentleman drivers of trotting horses in New York." He added: "Whenever possible he used to come up from the office early in the afternoon to drive in the park before dark. Many a day we children waited for him at the stable, for he was always glad to have one of us drive with him if we could."[15]

On these drives through the first major public park in the United States, he was experiencing the embodiment of the newly imported English ideals of how a park should look and how it should be used. When the Rockefellers moved to New York, Central Park was just about completed. Its designers, Frederick Law Olmsted and Albert Vaux, had envisioned a new kind of public space for Americans when they laid out the broad lawns, the sweeping drives, and carefully sited groves of trees. They intended that:

> In that area there would be space enough to have broad reaches of park and pleasure-grounds, with a real feeling of the breadth and beauty of green fields, the perfume and freshness of nature. . . . In such a park, the citizens who would take excursions in carriages, or on horseback, could have the substantial delights of country roads and country scenery, and forget for a time the rattle of the pavements and the glare of brick walls.[16]

It was in Central Park that JDR Jr. was first introduced to the idea of a park as public space, and to the concept that some time spent in nature was essential to the health and well-being of urban dwellers. His own childhood experiences confirmed this. During his school days in New York, when his health several times succumbed to urban pressures and the difficulties of being the only male heir to such a prominent name and fortune, he was sent back for part of the school year to Forest Hill, where the outdoor life and peace restored him.

Immediately after graduating from Brown University, he began to work at his father's offices in New York City. There he became immersed in complex business affairs, and he held major responsibilities for which he had virtually no preparation and no guidance. He worked very long hours during this trying time, but he kept his balance by returning to the outdoor skills and pleasures he had pursued as a boy. Chopping wood, for example, became an absorbing and wonderfully releasing pleasure for him after a long, grueling day:

> . . . in New York, he had truckloads of logs brought to his father's stable—logs about twenty feet long and one or two feet in diameter. Coming from his office in the late afternoon, and arming himself with a crossbuck saw, an ax, wedges, and a maul, he would cut and split the logs into proper length for firewood. "It was magnificent exercise," he said half a century later. "I did it for years. Then at the end of each session, I would run all the way home."[17]

In addition to this exercise, JDR Jr. drove himself to work every day in his carriage behind two handsome black horses. At a time when most men of means were intent on getting about in their new

In line with his belief in the benefits of the outdoors, JDR Jr. drove himself to his office in the city every day. (In 1913, when this photo was taken, gentlemen drove their own carriages, the coachman riding behind.) *Rockefeller Archive Center*

cars, this attracted considerable comment. One newspaper noted: "Automobiles appeal to the son of the richest man in the world when it comes to practical use, but for exercise and recreation he prefers horses. So his team calls for him every morning, and he drives it down to No. 26 Broadway, just as the old time New Yorkers used to do when taxicabs or even horse cars were not even dreamed of."[18] Another newspaper article commented: "Young Mr. Rockefeller believes in the out-of-door existence and advocates it at every opportunity, not only by speech but by action."[19]

Since the outdoor life had become such an essential part of his own life, JDR Jr. was well able to understand how important the outdoors could be for others. So, given the ideals and values in which he believed, it was not surprising that he wanted to make the natural world available to others who might not have the means to do so easily.

When still quite young, JDR Jr. had begun to explore the upper reaches of Manhattan and the lower Hudson River Valley on his own by horse or carriage. Fosdick noted:

He was deeply interested . . . in horseback riding and driving a span, and often, at the end of a pleasant spring or autumn day, he would be seen, perhaps in the company of one of his favorite cousins, Florence Briggs or Emma Rockefeller, driving in a Stanhope phaeton through Central Park, or up the Boulevard to where The Cloisters now stand [Fort Tryon], or across the Yonkers Ferry (generally on horseback) to explore the Palisades. He had been brought up with horses, and as time went on they became increasingly an indispensable factor in his recreation.[20]

On his rides up along the Hudson, he returned again and again to these places with grand vistas and picturesque beauty. Gradually he determined that when he grew up he would find a way to give these lands to the people of New York City. A newspaper article entitled "The Dream of a Boy" noted that on his rides to Fort Tryon he would say to himself, "Someday I'm going to buy all this land around here and give it to the city. Returning it so that everybody can enjoy it. This is a view that everyone ought to see."[21] After the Palisades cliffs had been conserved against further quarrying, he also acquired land along the top of the Palisades to protect it from the ravages of development and gave it to the state of New Jersey for a park. Years later, he did buy the Fort Tryon area of upper Manhattan and gave it to New York City for public use.

At the opening of Fort Tryon Park, the site of The Cloisters museum, his remarks expressed the same singleness of purpose and interest in the public weal that he later applied to the building of Acadia National Park:

> It gives me the greatest pleasure and satisfaction to know that from this day forth and for all time, Fort Tryon Park will be available for the enjoyment, the recreation and the health of the people of this land in which I have lived with them as neighbor and friend since early childhood. No place in Manhattan Island offers so much of natural beauty as the area. For nearly fifty years I have known and loved it. Almost twenty years have elapsed since I acquired the property with the sole purpose of making it a public park. It has been held ever since, pending the time when that purpose could best be carried out.
>
> And now as my dream is about to be realized, I am hoping two things. First, that this spot whose natural beauty has only been enhanced by the hand of man, may in the years to come bring as great happiness to you, the people of New York, as it has brought to me during the many years that have passed. Secondly, that you will cherish and preserve it with the same brooding care and untiring interest which has made it what it is today.[22]

In addition to the ideals of service and the belief in the importance of nature that JDR Jr. developed, his outlook on the world was being expanded by extensive travel, both in the western United States and in Europe. When he was ten, the family took a rail trip to the West. Two years later, they returned for another visit to Yellowstone. Yosemite and Yellowstone Park, set in the vast, open spaces of the West, offered a sense of the kind of scale possible for a national park and what could be done in a conservation effort. They were also a reminder that at the time there were no national parks east of the Mississippi.

Bicycle trips with friends through the countryside of England,

Wales, Holland, France, and Switzerland during his college years gave JDR Jr. the pleasure of discovering the architectural riches, urban parks, and particular landscapes of those countries. He was especially touched by the beauty of the English countryside and fascinated by the light shining through the stained-glass windows of the English cathedrals.

Riding and coaching were very popular forms of recreation for the well-to-do at the turn of the century, and they offered opportunities for many interesting trips in this country and abroad. By the time he was in his twenties, JDR Jr. had become as experienced in a carriage as he was on a horse. Tom Pyle, a longtime employee at Pocantico Hills, said of him: "Mr. Junior, like his father before him, was an expert driver—of either a pair or a four-in-hand. With the four-in-hand he was actually better than either the estate coachman or the head of the stable. . . ."[23] In 1901, shortly before his marriage to Abby Aldrich, he took a coaching trip through England, and in 1904 he and Abby took a coaching trip to the Berkshires and down the Hudson River. In 1906 they rode all through the Berkshires. Over the years they visited many resorts that had carriage trails for riding and driving. Their two favorite destinations seem to have been the Mohonk Mountain House in New York's Shawangunk Mountains and The Homestead in Hot Springs, Virginia.

Mohonk was a particularly appealing place to the senior Rockefellers, and their names as well as those of JDR Jr. and Abby appear in some of the old registers. Mohonk was developed by two Quaker brothers, Albert and Alfred Smiley, who not only loved the out-of-doors but also were strict prohibitionists whose religious beliefs forbade dancing and cards. They also espoused family and community values similar to those of the Rockefellers, and they ran their huge, rambling establishment like a home. But it is also a place of dramatic beauty that was carefully conserved for posterity by the Smileys, who gradually accumulated seven thousand acres of the mountainous land around their hotel. The carriage roads there, constructed mostly before the turn of the century, must have been inspiring and instructive to JDR Jr. Hewn out of the rocky crags of the Shawangunk Mountains, they were all hand-built by the Smileys with the same kind of care and attention to detail JDR Jr. was later to expend at Acadia. The early brochures for the inn extolled the variety and splendor of the views from the thirty-odd miles of carriage roads that JDR Jr. explored.

At The Homestead in Virginia, there are more than a hundred miles of carriage roads. It, too, was a family-run establishment, with a long tradition of southern hospitality. For years, JDR Jr. and Abby

JDR Jr. and Abby out for a drive in the phaeton at Pocantico Hills, 1912. Little David holds the reins.
Rockefeller Archive Center

JDR Jr. always took his favorite mount, Stephanie, to The Homestead at Hot Springs, Virginia. 1930s.
Rockefeller Archive Center

went there regularly for a two- to three-week spring holiday. He had his favorite horses sent ahead and loved to explore the mountain drives, bridle paths, and walks in the Warm Springs Valley.

In 1893, the year that JDR Jr. entered college, JDR Sr. began to buy land on the Hudson River near Tarrytown, about twenty-five miles north of New York City. The family's lives were more and more centered in New York, and it became difficult to find the time for the long journey to Forest Hill. Also, JDR Sr.'s brother William had bought property there and often spoke of the attractiveness of that part of the Hudson Valley. It was inviting to think they could have a country retreat within a day's travel of New York City. JDR Jr. was involved from the start in purchasing land with his father. In addition to the land immediately around the house that formed an enclosed estate of approximately three hundred acres, they gradually ac-

The carriage roads at Pocantico Hills, with their bridges and coping stones, were precursors to the roads JDR Jr. built on Mount Desert Island. *Rockefeller Archive Center*

quired more than three thousand acres of the surrounding rolling farmlands and woods.

Pocantico Hills, as the new estate came to be called, provided JDR Jr. with a vast landscape for exercising his own considerable but untested design and building skills for the first time. As soon as the newly acquired house had been readied for the family, they of course began to build carriage roads. Although JDR Sr. laid out the early roads, and he and his son worked together on some of them, JDR Jr. did the major portion on his own. The result was fifty-five miles of horse roads winding through the property. It was also at Pocantico, on the lands outside the estate, that JDR Jr. first expanded his father's concept of building roads for personal pleasure. Even though he retained ownership of this park during his lifetime, its carriage roads were open to the public for walking, riding, and carriage driving from the moment they were built.

The work on the carriage roads at Pocantico Hills began shortly before those in Maine, providing a period of experience and experimentation, but most of the road building occurred simultaneously in both places. Because he owned the land in Pocantico Hills, JDR Jr. did not have to answer to anyone except himself. He could plan, lay out, and build the roads as he saw fit.

All of JDR Jr.'s background culminated in his deep understanding that all people, especially those in cities, need access to open space in order to survive the tensions of modern life, and in his firm belief that "nature's treasure store of beauty" can make people's lives "happier, richer, better."[24] Olmsted's work on Central Park simply put into a practical context what JDR Jr. understood and believed in as a builder: that roads and paths were needed to give access to open space. Pocantico was also a model of a great park that he could use to shape his vision for Acadia, and his work on the Pocantico roads gave him the personal experience he needed to take on a project of the magnitude of Acadia National Park.

CHAPTER 2

The Inspiration of the Place

Mount Desert Island is one of those places that catch your breath and then catch your heart and won't let go. Its mountains and seashore, rich in land life and sea life, invited exploration, contemplation, and exploitation from the earliest times. Successive cultures—Indian, French, and English—summered there to reap the benefits of the natural resources. Some came to claim land for their governments. Eventually, the island's magic touched the hearts of enough people so that a long process of conservation began. This complex history set the stage for the role of John D. Rockefeller, Jr., in the development of Acadia National Park and its unique carriage roads.

The first Europeans arrived by water, as had the Indians before them. Today, most vacationers arrive by land, driving across the causeway from the mainland near Trenton. But in either case, it is the mountains that present themselves first. They rise up at the edge of the sea, tinged blue in the atmosphere, startling the gaze by their unexpectedness. Their tops have been worn and rounded by ancient glaciers, giving them a mild and almost personable aspect—but they are massive and commanding at the same time. On closer approach, colors and forms become more apparent. Rosy hues of granite dominate their peaks, and varying shades of green forest form mantles upon their slopes. The ever-present underlying granite disappears under the trees and reappears at the shoreline.

The island pleasantly assails all the senses, but the sense of smell is the first to succumb. The air is incredibly fresh and clean, perfumed by the sea and the odors of the evergreen forests. Prevailing winds carry these scents all across the island.

The abundance of natural life on the island is overwhelming. Freshwater lakes lie hidden in the mountains within the island's heart—a wonderful surprise so close to the sea. Surrounded by forest or meadow, the lakes are clear and unpolluted, and the island's insistent ocean rhythm is here replaced by the lap of little waves. Inland birds are audible on every side, and there is great variety of vegetable and animal pond life.

Opposite: **The S.S. *Mount Desert* steams out of Seal Harbor in the 1880s. *Seal Harbor Historical Society***

31

Mount Desert Island seen from Islesford, about 1912. *Southwest Harbor Public Library*

The forested parts of the island are both unusual and luxuriant. The northern and temperate climatic zones meet and overlap on Mount Desert, so there is abundant plant life and wildlife characteristic of both zones, and the island is a veritable paradise for scientist, artist, and ordinary visitor.

Whether in the first blush of spring with the wild plum and wild cherry tinting the edge of the woods, or the last riot of fall with the brilliant reds and yellows of maple and birch set against the dark greens of the conifers, the scene is captivating. Even when the landscape is shrouded in the densest fog, there is a kind of magic as the forms of trees, rocks, and shoreline slip in and out of view and the buoys sound their mournful warnings to passing ships.

Mount Desert has the only mountain range on the Eastern Seaboard. In the dim past, more than 500 million years ago, silt accumulated to a great depth on the floor of ancient seas and over time hardened into rock. Volcanic action forced the rock up into high peaks, many thousands of feet higher than today's mountains. Over eons, these peaks were worn down by glacial action, and new seas rose around them, new deposits of silt accumulated, and the process was repeated. These events left the remnants of two layers of sedimentary rock known as the Ellsworth Schist and Bar Harbor series, plus a layer of volcanic material known as the Cranberry Island series. These formations were disrupted again and again by massive upheavals of molten rock (magma), which formed the three types of granite that predominate on the island today: fine-grained, medium-grained, and coarse-grained.

Then, over the next few million years, a succession of twenty to thirty ice sheets passed over the Northeast from Canada, grinding the mountain range lower and lower. The retreat of the latest glacier, eleven thousand years ago, left the terrain that is visible today. Long fingers of ice wedged their way between the mountains, scouring out deep crevices that today contain the lakes of Mount Desert. In one place the ice bore in so deeply that the crevice formed Somes Sound—the only true fjord on the East Coast of the United States— a four-mile finger of water bounded on both sides by sheer rock walls. Since the glaciers descended from the north, their action rounded off the mountains on their northern sides but left the southern slopes jagged and precipitous. They left debris in their wake, randomly depositing large boulders like the notable one perched on the east face of South Bubble Mountain. As the glaciers finally retreated, the land rose, released from the tremendous pressure and weight, and the sea advanced, filling the crevices and valleys between the high peaks, creating Mount Desert Island and its many smaller satellites.

Many more thousands of years were needed for adequate soils to build up to support the diverse plant life now found on the island. The predominantly acid soils derive from granite, but there are also pockets of sweeter or even limey areas derived from the remnants of earlier metamorphic rock. The forest that clothes large areas of the mountains and valleys comprises pine, spruce, and balsam fir. On some north-facing slopes are also a few places where hemlock grows. Interspersed with the conifers are various hardwoods, including several species of maple, birch, beech, scrub oak, and mountain ash. Many smaller flowering trees and shrubs, such as wild cherry, wild plum, and witch hazel, enrich the mix of colors and textures. Innumerable wildflowers, ferns, and mosses carpet large areas of the island. *The Silva of North America* (1897) described Mount Desert from the perspective of the botanist:

> Wild flowers are abundant from early spring when the Trailing Arbutus or Mayflower puts forth its blossoms, till the Witch Hazel blooms in fall, scattering as it flowers its long-held seed. Orchids of the terrestrial

species grow freely in beautiful and interesting forms, culminating in display at mid-summer in the superb Fringed Orchid with its pale purple flowers. The pure white Trillium with deep purple blotches, the Clintonia, forming great beds of splendid foliage in the woods, the Wild Iris and the Cardinal Flower along the banks of streams, the native Lilies, growing among beds of ferns, the decorative Twisted Stalk with brick-red, pendant fruit, the Hairbell, clinging to cliffs and ledges by the sea, the summer Roses and the autumn Asters, the Blueberries and Wild Strawberries, the Raspberries and Blackberries, the Shad Bush and the Thorn, the Viburnum, most beautiful of northern woodland shrubs, the Rhodora, sung by Emerson, the Sumach and the Mountain Ash—there is no period the season through that lacks its special interest of flower or fruit.[1]

This rich display combines arctic and subarctic plants with others from farther south that reach their northern limit on the island. This broad palette was appreciated and drawn upon by JDR Jr. as he planned the plantings for his Acadia carriage roads.

The forest floor is a fairy carpet, a miniature replica of the larger universe around it. It is composed of myriad elements whose colors, textures, and shapes offer almost infinite variety. The various mosses form carpets or little mounds of emerald green, and ferns of all sizes are intermingled with blueberry bushes, bunchberry, wintergreen, and other creeping plants. Lichens and fungi grow on the rocks and deadfall in their own palette of grays, oranges, and yellow-greens, with touches of scarlet on the upright clusters familiarly known as prussian soldiers.

Waterfalls tumble down the mountainsides into streams meandering through the forest, catching the light, splashing, foaming, or burbling on to the sea. The woodland vistas are grand and intimate by turns. The poet, painter, and photographer can find as much delight in this landscape as the geologist, botanist, and ornithologist.

And surrounding all is the sea. Several sand beaches promise shell hunting, sunbathing, sandcastle building, and even a swim for the hardy. There are still octogenarians (my mother among them) who maintain that a daily morning swim in the frigid waters is certain to stimulate health and increase longevity. The local fishermen, however, have a dimmer view of the dark, cold water, and, as a matter of fact, most of them cannot swim. Most of the shoreline is rocky, interspersed with wonderful beaches carpeted with small stones of all shapes and colors. Inevitably they find their way into pockets and summer cottages along with that particular child's delight, sea glass. Along the shore, the granite's long, sloping ledges have fissures and crevices, marvelous places to explore the life of the sea at low tide. Barnacles, various mollusks, starfish, sea shrimp, crabs, and many species of seaweed inhabit the tidal pools formed by the ledges and invite contemplation. The ledges are also ideal for climbing and scrambling, racing the waves, and soaking up the sun.

Over it all, the sky arches. On Mount Desert there is a wonderful sense of spaciousness, and the mountaintops afford an infinite variety of views: out to sea, over the island, or back toward the mainland.

"L'Isle de Mont Desert," as Samuel de Champlain, the early French explorer of New France, named it, appears to have been inhabited first more than five thousand years ago by an ancient fishing culture now referred to as the Tuna people. (Champlain's diary explains that the mountaintops of the island had no trees, so he used the French word *desert*, meaning bare or devoid of vegetation.) The first known summer visitors, archaeologists tell us, were the Abnaki Indians.[2] For centuries before the Europeans came, they arrived with their families in early summer and stayed until the fall harvest and hunt. Sargent Collier, a park historian, has written this account of their visits:

> There is a distinct parallel between the Indians who frequented Mount Desert and the later summer visitors. The Indians considered summers spent here the most agreeable part of their lives. They, with considerable justification, regarded the island as a health resort and brought along their old people from the mainland to build up their strength against the winter.
>
> In spring they loaded the family canoe and paddled out to set up bark wigwams on the same lot as the previous year. Then they settled down to dig clams and fish and to enjoy a good measure of leisure.
>
> At a date roughly conforming to our day-after-Labor-Day, they returned to their palisaded winter villages at Kadesquit, on the Penobscot [River] near present day Bangor.[3]

The arrival of increasing numbers of Europeans was not so peaceful. The island became the subject of a protracted dispute between the English and the French. For nearly a hundred years (until the 1770s), this hostility effectively discouraged any real settlement. By then the English had become the dominant presence and the French had formally ceded the island to them. During the period of conflict, the Abnaki peoples were gradually pushed out of their ancestral lands, and for a long period the island had no summer visitors.

Between 1770 and 1850, settlement of the island began in earnest as individuals and families migrated north and east along the coast. A strong local community developed with a varied and successful economy based on timbering, shipbuilding, fishing, and quarrying the fine local granite. By 1870, most of the virgin timber was gone. Ships were being built in towns such as Southwest Harbor and Bass Harbor. Hall Quarry on Somes Sound was shipping granite all across the United States for street paving blocks and building construction. Herring and sardines were being canned, and the island was dotted with many small farms. People with such names as Fernald, Simpson, Candage, and Clement became the backbone of island life. From sturdy families such as these, JDR Jr. would later recruit stonemasons, engineers, contractors, nurserymen, and laborers to build the carriage roads.

In 1844, a visitor arrived whose enthusiasm was profoundly to affect the future of the island. He was Thomas Cole, an early leader of the Hudson River School of painters and a writer as well. Having come to explore the island and to paint, Cole was captivated by the drama and beauty of the place, and he soon spread the word among his friends. Other painters, including Frederick Edwin Church, quickly followed. The prose and the paintings of this artistic vanguard were in great measure responsible for stirring interest in Mount Desert as a vacation spot. A 1921 National Park Service brochure described an entry from the diary of Charles Tracy, the father of Mrs. J. Pierpont Morgan, depicting an early island outing that included Frederick Church:

> The party was a large one—26 in all—and filled Somes's Tavern to overflowing. . . . They climbed the mountains, tramped through the woods, lost themselves in them—half a dozen of them—and slept by a campfire in the wild; drove over to Bar Harbor, then on to Schooner Head, where they slept at the old farmhouse, climbing the then nameless "mountain with the cliff" that shadowed it at sundown, and drinking by the pitcherful such milk as New York could not supply and then like Hans Breitman, in climax to their stay they gave a party, importing by the boat to Southwest Harbor the first piano the island had ever seen and inviting to it the islanders and fisher folk from far and near. It was a great success. They danced, they sang songs, thay played games, and had a lobster salad such as only millionaires can have to-day, keeping up their gayety until 2 o'clock in the morning, when their last guests—two girls from Bar Harbor who had driven themselves over for it—hitched up their horse and left for home in spite of remonstrance and the offer of a bed. Such was the beginning of Mount Desert social life.[4]

After the artists came the scientists, especially botanists and geologists, to study the rich flora and fauna and the rock formations. Following them came professional families—clergy, physicians, academics—as well as the families of Bangor and Boston businessmen. They were people who did not object to the rustic accommo-

dations then available and who loved the woods, mountains, and lakes of Mount Desert as they were. Among these early vacationers were Charles W. Eliot, Harvard's young president, and Joseph Curtis, a landscape architect. They were among the first of this new influx of summer visitors to buy property and build at Northeast Harbor on the east side of the island. Of these two, Charles Eliot became one of the principal figures in the subsequent efforts to conserve the land. Providentially, Charles Eliot also became a mentor and friend to JDR Jr., and they maintained close touch during the building of the carriage roads until Eliot's death in 1924. They first met when President Eliot was asked by JDR Jr. to join the board of the Rockefeller Foundation shortly after it was formed in 1903. (Eliot also served on the General Education Board and the International Health Board, charitable endeavors both established by the Rockefellers.) At the time, Eliot was in his seventies and JDR Jr. was in his late twenties, yet the two developed a strong mutual admiration and friendship. Eliot not only offered advice on foundation matters but also strongly defended JDR Jr. during his most difficult times, including the early period of controversy over the carriage roads.

Meanwhile, Bar Harbor, on the northeast side of Mount Desert facing Frenchman Bay, was attracting increasing numbers of sum-

Bar Harbor in the 1870s boasted several immense summer hotels. *Bar Harbor Historical Society*

mer folk. Rude taverns were replaced by hotels in the 1870s, and eventually the wealthier visitors began to construct summer cottages. As early as the 1860s, regular steamship service operated from Portland and Rockland to Southwest Harbor and Bar Harbor. By 1877, fast train service was available from Boston to Hancock Point, where Maine Central Railroad steamers met the train and took passengers on to all of the island's major resort towns. In 1882, steamship service came to Seal Harbor. Soon people were flocking to the area from all the large Eastern Seaboard cities.

Inevitably the character of the summer clientele began to change. The plainer folk were succeeded by those of "wealth and taste," and they in turn attracted multimillionaires "fleeing from life's complications," as Samuel Eliot Morison put it.[5] More and more property was bought up along the Frenchman Bay shorefront. The "summer cottages" being built were in fact elaborate mansions in disguise. By the 1880s, Bar Harbor had become one of the summer social capitals of the United States, with all the attendant bustle and activity typical of other adult playgrounds. There were horse races, yacht races, dances, and, of course, an elaborate and extensive social schedule.

The Summit Hotel on Green (now Cadillac) Mountain, about 1886. To the right of the hotel is a U.S. signal station tower. *Bar Harbor Historical Society*

The island's popularity hastened the need for conservation measures. Not only was the shorefront increasingly sought for development, the mountaintops and lake frontage were being eyed as well. The very features that made the island attractive were increasingly in danger of being destroyed by heedless enthusiasm and greed. The peak of Cadillac, highest mountain on the island, was bought by an enterprising gentleman for commercial development. Not only did he build a rough road to the top and construct a series of hotels there in the early 1880s, he had a cog railway constructed so his guests could ride up and down in comfort and gaze upon the view he was defacing. (The enterprise eventually went bankrupt, and the hotel was torn down in 1896.)

Cadillac Mountain (or Green Mountain, as it was known then), the highest peak on the Eastern Seaboard, rises some 1,527 feet. From its summit, there are superb views over all the rest of the island. Looking northwest toward the mainland from its peak, you can see Katahdin, the tallest mountain in Maine. Cadillac's splendid pink and gray granite shoulders are visible from all over the region. The ungainly hotel, and the six-thousand-foot cog railway carrying tourists up to it, were an intrusion that completely changed the character of the mountain and its surrounding viewpoints. Nature's graceful curves were disrupted by man's harsh horizontals and verticals.

In addition to the damage resulting from overdevelopment, there were potential problems created by advancing technology. The invention of the portable sawmill could have opened up the farthest reaches of mountain and gorge to timbering interests. As Richard Hale pointed out in *The Story of Bar Harbor*, "As long as saws were water driven, or steam-engine driven, saw mills stayed on low ground, and it was uneconomical to cut wood on high hills. . . . But gasoline power saws could be taken higher up, and the last stands of good timber were on the mountains. . . ."[6] Areas that before had been inaccessible suddenly were all within reach. Large tracts on the east side of the island were already owned by lumber interests. Mount Desert stood in danger of being denuded of its forest cover, the essential outer skin of this vulnerable environment.

Fortunately, some of the year-round and summer people recognized the negative potential of the portable sawmill as well as the problems brought about by the island's rising popularity and its attendant real estate boom. These prescient folk tended to be the ones who loved the island as it had been in its simpler and more rustic days. Foremost among them was President Charles W. Eliot of Harvard.

A cog railway brought tourists to the top of Cadillac Mountain from 1883 to 1887, following a precipitous route. *Bar Harbor Historical Society*

It was to the village improvement societies that Eliot turned for support when he decided to form an organization to defend Mount Desert's special beauty. Here gathered the civic-minded and concerned citizens, those most likely to be sympathetic to the conservation issues beginning to be discussed. By the early 1900s, nearly all of the local townships had their own village improvement societies—organizations formed to carry out community tasks deemed important by both summer and year-round citizens. These societies arose in true New England fashion in response to the limitations of small town governments that had neither the funds nor the manpower to carry out many necessary services. They addressed a wide range of issues—from sanitary concerns to the public appearance of the towns.

The improvement societies also formed special committees to carry out particular functions. The Bridle Path Committee of Northeast Harbor, for instance, was established to plan, build, and maintain riding trails for the pleasure and enjoyment of the summer vacationers. Path committees sprang up to build and maintain the island's woodland trails, which were extensions of paths built by eighteenth-century settlers to link their houses with the first roads and with the sea. In the 1870s, the summer folk began to extend these old paths into the mountainous interior areas, and there were more than 250 miles of trails by 1915.[7]

Eliot decided to assemble a small group of these interested people to discuss the formation of a trusteeship that would buy and hold land in order to preserve some of the island's most spectacular and fragile areas. Included at this meeting were members of the village improvement societies of Seal Harbor, Northeast Harbor, and Bar Harbor. Eliot also invited his Boston friend George B. Dorr (who brought along George Vanderbilt and John S. Kennedy, a New York banker of some means). The Episcopal bishop of Massachusetts, William Lawrence, who later opposed JDR Jr.'s road work, was there as well. The idea for this conservation organization had come from Eliot's son, Charles Eliot, Jr. A landscape architect and ardent conservationist, the younger Eliot had earlier founded a similar organization, the Massachusetts Trustees of Public Reservations, which had successfully preserved lands around Boston. Introduced to Mount Desert Island by his father in the 1870s, young Eliot loved its rustic simplicity and wildness.[8]

On August 12, 1901, the Hancock County Trustees of Public Reservations (HCTPR) was formed, with Charles Eliot as president, George Dorr as director, George Stebbins as treasurer, and the firm of Deasy and Lynam, of Bar Harbor, as legal counsel. Robert Lynam

**George Bucknam Dorr
devoted years of his life and
most of his personal fortune
to the development of
Acadia National Park.** *Bar
Harbor Historical Society*

agreed to be secretary. In the years that followed, all of these men
worked tirelessly to protect the island and to create a public park.
After JDR Jr. became active in the island's preservation, some of
them helped him to purchase property and to negotiate rights-of-
way over private land.

It could not be known at that time how pivotal a figure George
Dorr would become. Here was a man who had found his true cause.
From the time of his first involvement with the Hancock County
Trustees of Public Reservations in 1901 until his death forty-three
years later, Dorr devoted himself singlemindedly and often
singlehandedly to the cause of preserving Mount Desert Island's
scenic beauty. He was a wealthy bachelor from Boston, the sole heir
of a textile fortune; his parents, among the first summer residents of
the island, built the second summer cottage in Bar Harbor in 1868.
Known as "the Father of Acadia National Park" in recognition of his
tireless efforts,[9] Dorr contributed not only his time and energy but
also his personal wealth. He used most of his inheritance for the
building of the park, and he tirelessly urged others to support these
efforts. In fact, without his constant vigilance, his willingness to give
top priority to the HCTPR program, and his ability to drop everything
on behalf of his vision, it is doubtful whether Acadia National Park
would exist today in anything close to its present scale and quality.

Dorr's first task was to secure a charter for the fledgling
organization and ensure its tax-exempt status. On January 1, 1903,
the Maine Legislature granted a charter that included the following
statement of purpose: ". . . to acquire, by devise, gift or purchase, and
to own, arrange, hold, maintain or improve for public use lands in
Hancock County, Maine, which by reason of scenic beauty, historical
interest, sanitary advantage or other like reasons may become
available for such purpose."[10]

The Hancock County Trustees of Public Reservations received
two small gifts of property at its inception, but it was between 1908
and 1913 that a significant number of gifts and purchases were made.
With the financial help of banker John S. Kennedy, the generous gifts
of many other summer residents, and his own resources, Dorr was
able to acquire five thousand acres of prime property, including the
summit of Cadillac Mountain, Otter Cliffs, Sieur de Monts Spring, and
Eagle Lake. He also donated some of the property he had inherited
from his father. George Stebbins, one of the first summer residents
of Seal Harbor as well as a founding member of the HCTPR, summed
up this remarkable achievement in his reminiscences of Seal Harbor:
"Few people realize, except those immediately concerned, that
these acquisitions were made just in time to save our forests from
being devastated by the wood cutters. . . . In acquiring these tracts

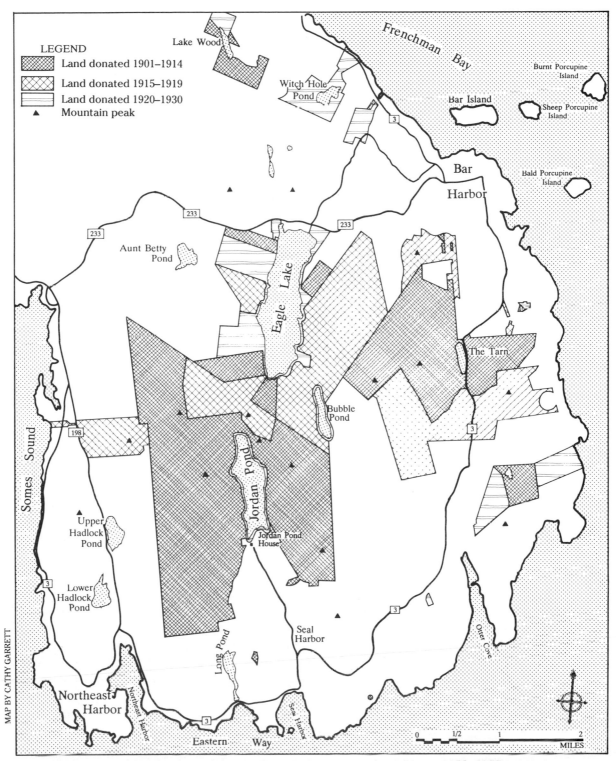

LEGEND

- Land donated 1901–1914
- Land donated 1915–1919
- Land donated 1920–1930
- ▲ Mountain peak

Frenchman Bay

Lake Wood

Witch Hole Pond

Burnt Porcupine Island

Bar Island

Sheep Porcupine Island

Bar Harbor

Bald Porcupine Island

Aunt Betty Pond

Eagle Lake

The Tarn

Bubble Pond

Somes Sound

Upper Hadlock Pond

Lower Hadlock Pond

Jordan Pond

Jordan Pond House

Seal Harbor

Otter Cove

Long Pond

Northeast Harbor

Northeast Harbor

Eastern Way

Seal Harbor

MILES

0   1/2   1   2

Map 1: Hancock County Trustees of Public Reservations Land Acquisitions, 1901–1930

for the reservations, thus saving the forests, we in some cases got ahead of the speculators and lumbermen by a few hours only."[11]

There was every reason to think that the future of the island was more secure when suddenly, in January 1913, Dorr received word that the Maine Legislature was about to consider a bill to rescind the charter of the HCTPR, a move that would render useless all the work accomplished so far. Dorr acted at once, using his personal contacts and skill to head off the revocation. Although contemporary accounts do not identify the forces behind the bill, it is hard not to suspect that lumber and real estate interests were somehow involved in this episode.[12]

This narrow escape gave birth to the idea of Acadia National Park. As Dorr himself put it, "It is here the story of our National Park begins, born of the attack upon our Public Reservations charter."[13] Dorr decided that in order to protect the preserve he and the HCTPR members had labored so hard to build, the lands should be under government protection and ownership. So, early in 1914, after convincing Eliot and the other trustees of the importance of his idea, he went to Washington to try to get the preserve accepted by the government as a park. After nearly two years of negotiation and what must have seemed interminable delay, due to the First World War, President Woodrow Wilson signed a proclamation declaring the establishment of the Sieur de Monts National Monument on July 8, 1916.

On August 25 of the same year, the National Park Service was formed, and Dorr saw his chance to further secure the protected lands of Mount Desert by having them designated a national park. This required an act of Congress, and, because of congressional preoccupation with the war effort, it took years of ingenuity to achieve. Not until February 26, 1919, did the Sieur de Monts National Monument become Lafayette National Park. Dorr had recognized that congressmen needed a way to identify with the new park in order to vote for its designation, and the Marquis de Lafayette's memory was very much present as Americans went to the defense of freedom in France. So the national monument that had been named for an early French explorer became a national park named for the Frenchman most celebrated as a sympathizer and supporter of the American Revolution. With the park's future secured, Dorr wrote, "The task that I had set myself to do six years before was done."[14]

In 1929, the park received its present name. World War I was over, and the name Lafayette no longer served to enlist support for the park that Dorr continued to pursue. He chose a new name with roots in both the Indian and the French heritage of the island. *La*

Cadie or *L'Acadie* is the French version of an Indian word meaning "the place."

All of these efforts had made Acadia National Park a legal fact, if not a working park, when JDR Jr. arrived in the summer of 1908. JDR Jr. and Abby were expecting their third child. Her physician summered in Blue Hill, a town just west of Mount Desert Island, and he suggested that the Rockefellers spend the summer in Bar Harbor, since he could easily get there for the birth. Perhaps remembering the island's charm from his first visit in 1893, during college days, JDR Jr. took that advice and rented a cottage in Bar Harbor for his young family. Their son Nelson (my father) was born there on August 8. Years later, JDR Jr. wrote in a letter to the *Bar Harbor Times:* "As a result of the summer thus spent on Mount Desert Island we were so enamored of its beauty that we returned the following year and the year after to occupy rented houses in Seal Harbor and then bought our present home there where we have been ever since."[15]

In 1910, they bought the piece of property he referred to, a 150-acre plot on Barr Hill above Seal Harbor that he called The Eyrie. Seal Harbor was on the quieter, less developed side of the island, away from the hustle and bustle of Bar Harbor. The summer folk in Seal Harbor tended to be professionals and intellectuals who were less inclined toward elaborate parties and social activities. The property

The original house at The Eyrie as it looked when JDR Jr. purchased it in 1910.
Rockefeller Archive Center

The Eyrie, after being expanded and remodeled by JDR Jr., seen from Long Pond, Seal Harbor. *Rockefeller Archive Center*

looked out over the Eastern Way to the south and back toward Sargent and Jordan mountains to the north. A moderate-sized house stood looking out to sea on granite ledges, with pine forest behind it. JDR Jr. again had selected a spot of great beauty with a house on the highest point of the land and commanding sweeping views—as he had done in Pocantico Hills and as his father had done in Forest Hill.

Just after the turn of the century, it was still quite difficult to get to Mount Desert Island, requiring a long journey by train or steamship and coach. Its very remoteness assured my grandparents a modicum of cherished privacy. With its varied natural terrain, spectacular views, and rich vegetation, it appealed to JDR Jr.'s sense of beauty and his love of nature. Here there were fewer people, more spaces, and plenty of unspoiled land available to buy and develop for himself and his family. Another attraction was the fact that automobiles were not allowed on the island. That meant he could engage in his favorite pastime and explore the island by horse and carriage without fear of disruption by the noisy and still crude gas-guzzler that had made his name a synonym for wealth.

JDR Jr. was under a tremendous burden of business responsibility when he first visited Maine and during the years when he was building the carriage roads. Between 1901 and 1910, his father had gradually retired from the management of the Standard Oil Company and all his other business commitments, leaving JDR Jr. more and more in charge. His father's early retirement thrust JDR Jr. into positions of great responsibility and personal risk. Although he was relatively young and inexperienced and had had little training for the perils of the corporate world, he was placed on a large number of corporate boards to represent his father's interests. Then, too, during that first decade of the twentieth century, a seemingly endless number of unrelenting attacks were leveled at the Standard Oil Company and its founder, JDR Sr.—and thus at JDR Jr. Sparked primarily by Ida Tarbell's important, highly critical book, *The History of the Standard Oil Company*, and fueled by other writers and the press, JDR Sr.'s critics saw him as the symbol of all the perceived evils of the capitalist system in America. Since his father steadfastly refused to respond to any public attacks, JDR Jr. had to stand by and watch his beloved father being vilified. The press inevitably included him in their attacks as well. Every day critical magazine and newspaper articles appeared. Even the Baptist men's Bible class JDR Jr. had taught for eight years—where he devotedly offered his own personal beliefs about daily living—was infiltrated by hostile reporters and brought into the public eye for ridicule. During the same period, JDR Jr. was called to serve on a special grand jury to investigate prostitution and white slave traffic in New York City, and was elected as its chairman, which brought him further into the public eye.

A firm believer in Prohibition, he became deeply engaged in the temperance movement, traveling around the country for speaking engagements. In addition, he spent a tremendous amount of time working with the Reverend Frederick Gates (hired in 1891 by JDR Sr. to assist with philanthropic enterprises) to create the three great foundations mandated by his father: the General Education Board, the Rockefeller Institute for Medical Research, and the Rockefeller Foundation. Beyond this, he was engaged in a host of other philanthropic projects, such as the Rockefeller Sanitary Commission, a project of the Rockefeller Foundation, which became responsible for the eradication of hookworm disease in the South. Someone less resolute than he or without the same deep sense of personal duty to family and society would surely have gone under. No wonder Maine's calm and remoteness were appealing.

In 1910, the year he and Abby bought their property in Maine, JDR Jr. made what he later termed "one of the most important decisions of my life."[16] He decided to redirect his life's work from being manager of his father's vast business interests to being a philanthropist. After working for his father for more than ten years and carefully studying the various facets of the family business, he realized that he had no desire to pursue his father's business interests or to make more money. He recognized that his heart and his imagination were captured by the possibility of what he could do in philanthropic endeavors, and he resolved to follow that course. He began to sever his relations with the many companies where he held directorships and devoted himself to a single focus: "The social purposes to which a great fortune could be dedicated." And he fulfilled this vision with extraordinary dedication and skill in the subsequent years.[17]

JDR Jr.'s work on the carriage roads at Acadia National Park was one of his great philanthropic projects and his first major conservation effort, but it satisfied a far more personal need. It was a project where all of his beliefs and sensibilities could be expressed, where professional interests and personal energies could meet. He could be with his family without interruptions, away from business obligations and the press. Here he could have his own pleasures and offer something back to the larger community by building public carriage roads. Here was a place that nourished his deep love of the land and its natural beauty. Here he could enjoy the outdoors in the ways he liked—horseback riding, carriage driving, picnicking, and walking through the exquisitely beautiful landscape. Given his firm beliefs in service and stewardship, and his commitment to philanthropy, there was no way he would fail to become involved in the local conservation efforts.

After his initial purchase of a house and land, JDR Jr. quickly engaged lawyer Albert H. Lynam of Bar Harbor, a relative of Robert Lynam, and began in his quiet fashion to purchase more land. His immediate interest was to secure the rest of Barr Hill, the land surrounding his house. Then he purchased Long Pond at the foot of the hill to the west. This protected his western view and gave him a lovely little body of fresh water for boating and swimming.

As far as I can tell from his private records, he apparently was working on his own until 1914. He continued to buy land discreetly, using A.H. Lynam and George Stebbins as his agents, and to build carriage roads for his own use. Then several events occurred that would profoundly change the future of JDR Jr.'s relationship to Mount Desert and the history of Acadia National Park.

The first of these events was related to that new technological wonder, the automobile. On the island, the car was perceived from the start as a mixed blessing. The summer folk were determined that the island should remain a refuge from it, but most of the year-round

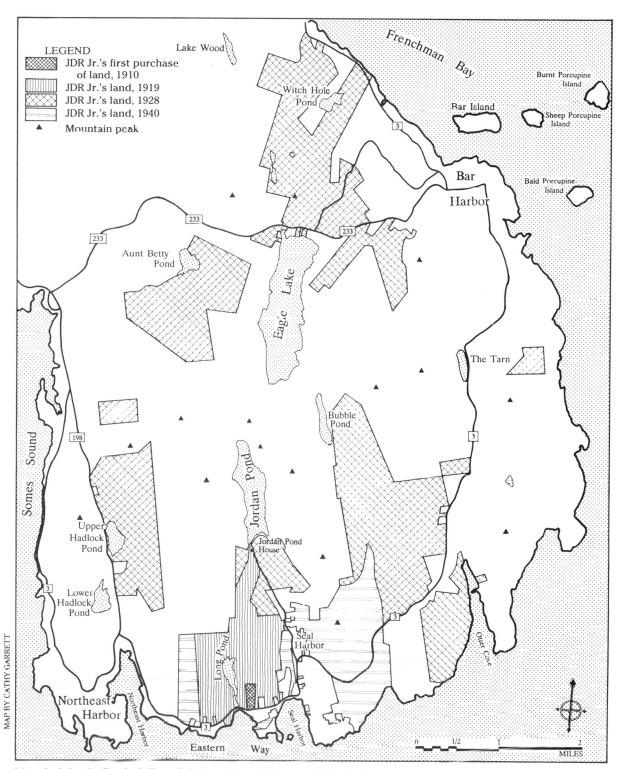

LEGEND
JDR Jr.'s first purchase
    of land, 1910
JDR Jr.'s land, 1919
JDR Jr.'s land, 1928
JDR Jr.'s land, 1940
▲ Mountain peak

Lake Wood
Frenchman Bay
Burnt Porcupine Island
Bar Island
Sheep Porcupine Island
Witch Hole Pond
Bald Porcupine Island
Bar Harbor
233
233
233
Aunt Betty Pond
Eagle Lake
The Tarn
3
Bubble Pond
Somes Sound
198
Jordan Pond
Upper Hadlock Pond
3
Lower Hadlock Pond
Jordan Pond House
Long Pond
Seal Harbor
3
Otter Cove
Northeast Harbor
Northeast Harbor
Seal Harbor
Eastern Way
3
0   1/2   1   2
MILES

Map 2: John D. Rockefeller, Jr.'s Land Acquisitions, 1910–1940

View across Eastern Way from Barr Hill, site of The Eyrie. *Rockefeller Archive Center*

residents who had to make a living in the area saw it as a very desirable advance and a good way to facilitate transport and daily activities. The issue was so heated that it ended up in the state legislature. At first, in 1908, the summer interests carried enough weight to sustain the ban on cars, but the debate continued, and in 1913 the commercial interests and year-round residents had gained enough support that the legislation was amended to allow cars only on the Bar Harbor side of the island. Seal Harbor and Northeast Harbor were still safe, as was JDR Jr.'s house. But it was just a matter of time until the last resistance was swept away, and that happened in 1915. The ubiquitous, noisy, smoke-belching autos began to roll over the causeway to the island in increasing numbers.

Without cars, Mount Desert had harkened back to the era when JDR Jr.'s life had been less hectic and less stressful—especially to the times at Forest Hill, the scene of his fondest childhood memories. Now this element was irrevocably lost. In no time, he knew, the regular island roads would be a mass of honking, puffing machinery, and it would become impossible to take the quiet rides he so enjoyed. Urban developments that made him ever wealthier were threatening the beautiful scenery of the island.

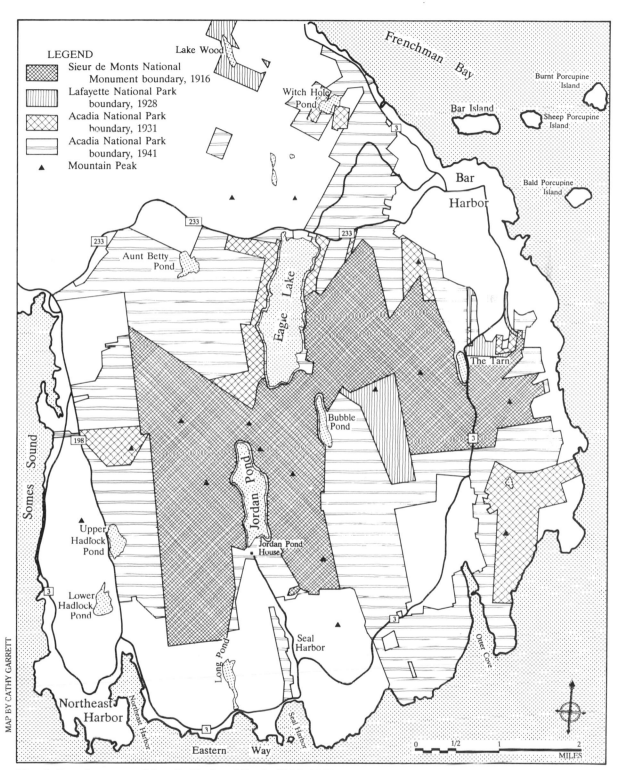

LEGEND

Sieur de Monts National
Monument boundary, 1916

Lafayette National Park
boundary, 1928

Acadia National Park
boundary, 1931

Acadia National Park
boundary, 1941

▲ Mountain Peak

Lake Wood

Frenchman Bay

Burnt Porcupine
Island

Witch Hole
Pond

Bar Island

Sheep Porcupine
Island

Bar

Harbor

Bald Porcupine
Island

233

233

Aunt Betty
Pond

Eagle Lake

The Tarn

Somes Sound

198

Bubble
Pond

Jordan Pond

3

Upper
Hadlock
Pond

Lower
Hadlock
Pond

Jordan Pond
House

3

Seal
Harbor

Otter Cove

Long Pond

Northeast
Harbor

Northeast Harbor

Seal Harbor

3

Eastern   Way

0   1/2   1   2

MILES

Map 3: Development of Acadia National Park, 1916–1941

On September 11, 1914, JDR Jr. received a letter from George Dorr introducing himself and asking for support for the endeavors of the HCTPR: "President Eliot has written me, as president of the Hancock County Trustees of Public Reservations, telling me of your interest in protecting and developing to public use the natural beauty of the Island, and promoting its welfare as a resort home. And he has advised me, as the Corporation's executive officer, to lay before you briefly its immediate and pressing need of funds which will enable it to secure the aid and cooperation of the Federal Government in its undertaking."[18] There is no record of a written answer to this request, but the two men met and began to work together soon thereafter, setting in motion a long collaboration and the beginning of JDR Jr.'s efforts toward creating a national park on Mount Desert Island.

During this time, JDR Jr. also began to conceive of building a much more extensive carriage-road system. The idea grew into a vision of making his roads available for public pleasure, recreation, and restoration in much the same way that they were for him. He would make a system to rival anything he had done before—for riders, carriage drivers, and pedestrians, for himself and other residents on the island:

> Believing that it [Acadia National Park] should ultimately extend to the ocean on one side and to Frenchmans Bay on the other and that access to it would be desirable not only for pedestrians but, in carefully chosen areas, for lovers of horses as well as automobilists, I began years ago buying lands on the Island having in mind to make possible the rounding out of the Park boundaries and its extension and development as above outlined.[19]

It was also "a virgin enterprise, and to a perfectionist like himself this meant that the work would not be hampered by the precedent of inferior standards nor would the scope of the project be limited by a preconceived plan." It was, in his words, "an ideal project."[20]

Thus, the beauty of the island, its magnetic appeal as a summer retreat and resort, the existence of the Hancock County Trustees of Public Reservations with George Dorr as its charismatic director, and the advent of the automobile—all conspired to invite the creation of Acadia National Park and the masterpiece known as "the Rockefeller Roads."

CHAPTER 3

The Road Work Begins

JDR Jr.'s Concept for the Carriage Roads

Moving through the scenery on the carriage roads at Acadia National Park feels natural and fluid—almost as if the roads had always been an integral part of the landscape. Their design is so subtle that the character of the land is revealed and experienced scene by scene. The roads bring you into relationship with your surroundings the moment you step out for a walk, and they engage you so thoroughly that the sequence of events predominates rather than the road. In fact, even though the casual visitor is probably not at all aware of any "design" as such, a tremendous amount of thought and planning was involved.

In building the Mount Desert Island carriage roads, JDR Jr. had in mind several specific objectives. On the simplest and most pragmatic level, he wanted to provide access to the island's mountains and valleys for riders on horseback and in carriages. Then, he wanted to open the inner regions of the landscape to larger numbers of pedestrians than those who used the many narrow footpaths already in existence. He understood that his carriage roads, with their smooth, wide surfaces, would make walking so much easier. He also wanted to connect the northern and southern sections of the park so it would extend from shore to shore. In short, he wished to make available to everyone the spectacular views of mountain and ocean, the vistas of lakes and forest, and the vignettes of meadows and woodland streams.

Underlying these objectives were his own very deep beliefs about the earth and our relationship to it. "I never had any doubt about the existence of a Divine being," he wrote to his biographer Fosdick. "To see a tree coming out in the spring was enough to impress me with the fact that God existed."[1]

"I think perhaps I have always had an eye for nature," he once commented. "I remember as a boy loving sunsets. I remember the sunsets from my bedroom window at 4 West Fifty-fourth Street, which looked west. I remember what the sycamore trees looked like and the maple trees. Every time I ride through the woods today, the smell of the trees—particularly when a branch has just been cut and

Opposite: **Riders passing under the Eagle Lake Bridge, 1930s.** *Bar Harbor Historical Society*

55

the sap is running—takes me back to my early impressions in the woods."[2]

JDR Jr.'s son Laurance also recalls his father's sensitivity to the land and his appreciation for the beauty in natural things. He described to me JDR Jr.'s keen awareness of each tree, waterfall, view, and contour as he moved about the landscape and his desire for others to experience what he experienced, as well as his amazement and delight when they did.[3] Dana Creel, one of JDR Jr.'s associates, was deeply touched by his reverence for nature and his belief that it could heal and enrich the inner being of humankind. He felt that JDR Jr.'s feelings were akin to those of the American Indian, in that he felt a deep personal responsibility for the preservation of the earth and understood the mutuality of our relationship—that we have a duty to care for her in return for what we receive, and not to abuse her. Creel remarked that JDR Jr. was always looking for the greatest oppportunity to experience the natural environment; everywhere he went, he made trails to take him outside into nature. He was not interested in photographing what he had seen, preferring to retain the visual memories in his mind, which is also characteristic of American Indian people.[4]

The methods JDR Jr. employed to carry out his objectives were deceptively simple, but they required a trained and sensitive eye, intimate knowledge of the terrain, and fine technical skills. The roads, designed to carry the walker or rider through the landscape by means of a sequence of "events," were laid out around these events, each carefully chosen to reveal the park's landscape to its greatest advantage.

Of uppermost importance were the views. JDR Jr. explored the mountains and valleys with intense interest to discover the vistas that best revealed the grandeur and beauty of this varied terrain, and he made sure that the roads connected these spots.

As a result, today it is possible to see the sun rise or set from these roads; to see back to the mainland and on a clear day discern distant Mount Katahdin; to see the sun shimmering on the ocean from the shoulder of Sargent Mountain; to behold the clouds reflected on Jordan Pond, one of the many lakes concealed within the mountains. The massive pink and gray granite underpinnings of the island become apparent as they are brought into view time and again in each different context.

The drive or walk around Eagle Lake on the carriage road, for example, combines several events and views of quite different character. Starting from the entrance, the first feature visible is Eagle Lake itself, more than two miles long and the second-largest lake on the island. A walk along the lake's northern shore reveals splendid

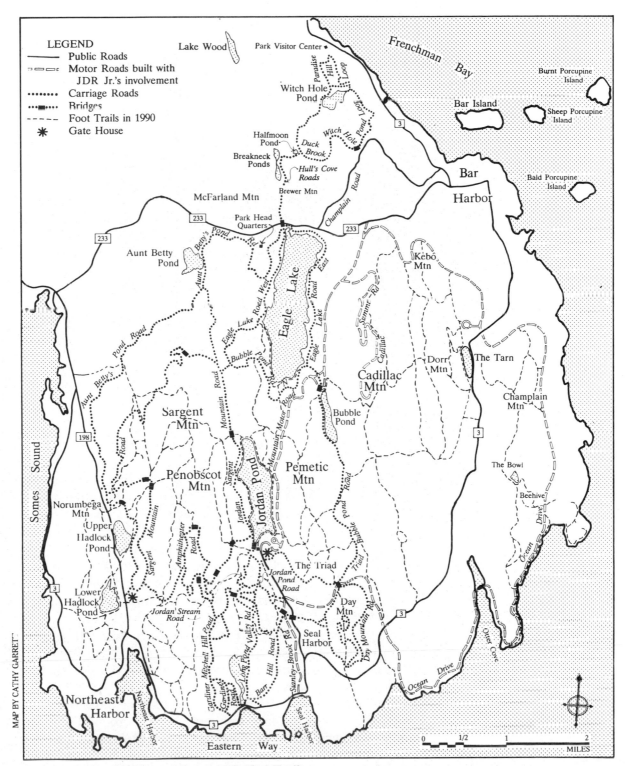

LEGEND
———— Public Roads
▭▭▭ Motor Roads built with JDR Jr.'s involvement
·········· Carriage Roads
·■·■·■· Bridges
– – – – Foot Trails in 1990
✳ Gate House

Lake Wood
Park Visitor Center
Frenchman Bay
Burnt Porcupine Island
Bar Island
Sheep Porcupine Island
Paradise Hill Loop
Witch Hole Pond
Bald Porcupine Island
Halfmoon Pond
Duck Brook
Witch Hole Pond Loop
Bar Harbor
Breakneck Ponds
Hull's Cove Roads
Brewer Mtn
McFarland Mtn
Champlain Road
Park Head Quarters
233
233
Aunt Betty Pond
Betty's Pond Rd
Kebo Mtn
Eagle Lake
Eagle Lake Road West
Eagle Lake Road East
Aunt Betty's Pond Road
Summit Rd
Eagle Lake
Cadillac
Bubble Pond
Dorr Mtn
The Tarn
Mountain Road
Cadillac Mtn
Champlain Mtn
Sargent Mtn
198
Bubble Pond
Mountain Motor Road
Pemetic Mtn
The Bowl
Sargent Mountain Road
Jordan Pond
Bubble Pond Road
Beehive
Penobscot Mtn
Amphitheater Road
Jordan
Sargent
3
Norumbega Mtn
Upper Hadlock Pond
The Triad
Triad
Jordan Pond Road
Day Mtn
Ocean Drive
Somes Sound
Lower Hadlock Pond
Jordan Stream Road
Gardiner Mitchell Hill Road
Long Pond Valley Rd
Barr Hill Road
Stanley Brook Rd
Seal Harbor
Day Mountain Road
Ocean Drive
Otter Cove
3
Northeast Harbor
Northeast Harbor
Gardiner Road
3
Seal Harbor
Ocean Drive
Eastern Way

0   1/2   1   2
MILES

Map 4: Carriage Roads and Connecting Foot Trails

views of Sargent and Jordan mountains to the south, and as the carriage road moves away from the lake along the eastern side, it is possible to look back down and enjoy its expanse. As JDR Jr. pointed out, "On general principles, one sees more of a lake by being a little higher up and not too close to its edge. The view, moreover, is usually more attractive if one looks down onto the lake from a little elevation [rather] than from practically the level of the lake. Then too, the road, further back and higher up, would undoubtedly be less apt to be seen from the lake. . . ."[5] Crossing the southern end of the lake, the road begins to climb toward Sargent Mountain, giving a prospect north toward Bar Harbor and Frenchman Bay. As the road descends again to the western side of the lake, a backward look over the water offers a lovely view of the Bubbles. Amid these larger views are innumerable vignettes of woods and shore and water that delight the eye and soothe the soul.

Other carriage roads lead the traveler through gentle curves in the woods and along the shores of lakes or streams. They traverse meadows and wander up toward mountain shoulders. The route leads through the dappled light of the woods, past mossy banks to a stream's edge or up the mountainside to a rushing waterfall, and on to startling views of ocean beyond. The element of surprise is not neglected; just when it seems that the woods have claimed the walk, the mountains beyond burst into view, and the roads take full advantage of the remarkable juxtaposition between the intimate and the grand that is so characteristic of Mount Desert.

From the beginning, there was no intention of establishing a hierarchy in the carriage-road system. Almost every road has grand views as well as a great variety of scenery. Brown Mountain Road, along the western base of Parkman and Sargent mountains, is perhaps the only one that does not seem to link any obvious points. However, it crosses several lovely streams and wanders through stands of hemlock and birch on the northern flanks of the two mountains, offering an intimate view of the surroundings. Just north of Sargent Mountain, it joins Aunt Betty Pond Road, which wanders through Gilmore Meadow and alongside Aunt Betty Pond. This area rewards the traveler with a great variety of views—over the meadow, back up toward Sargent Mountain, and out over Aunt Betty Pond and Eagle Lake. It combines a journey through the low-lying terrain with a slight climb for a backward look at the mountains.

The longest loop in the carriage-road system boasts a most spectacular series of events. Going all the way around Parkman, Sargent, and Penobscot mountains, a journey of more than eleven miles, it has seven bridges, each crossing a mountain stream, overlooking a waterfall, or traversing a deep ravine. There are vistas over the mountains and ocean in every direction, giving a tremendous sense of the scope of the scenery. Especially captivating is the view from Waterfall Bridge, where Hadlock Brook falls forty feet down the mountainside and then cascades over rocks and under the bridge before continuing on to Upper Hadlock Pond. Ferns and mosses cling to the damp rocks edging the stream, and the sun filtering through the trees creates shadow patterns on the road. If you climb down under the bridge, the stone structure makes a perfect frame for the dramatic waterfall. From here, continuing in a southerly direction, the road then begins to curve northeastward, climbing slightly through the woods until it emerges on the shoulder of Penobscot Mountain. At this point, the entire Western Way bursts into view, dotted with islands and the white sails of boats.

Despite their variety, the carriage roads never violate the island's mountaintops, leaving them to rise undisturbed out of the forest with their granite crowns untouched. Their heights are accessible only by narrow footpaths that are invisible from other vantage points and allow the visitor to slip almost unnoticed through the woods.

Originally, JDR Jr. planned only two major entrances to the carriage roads—one across from Brown Mountain on the western side of Route 3 and the other near Jordan Pond. His intention was to allow carriages to enter from the motor roads and to keep automobiles out. Each of these entrances was marked by a gate house, where a park attendant lived to maintain the gate. But in the early 1930s, before he gave the gate houses to the park, JDR Jr. installed his engineer, Paul Simpson, and his family in the Jordan Pond gate house. Paul's son, Charles, today recalls swinging on the gate when it had bells on it to signal that someone was passing through.[6] As the use of carriages declined, these gate houses became more and more a visual element rather than a practical one. Today, hikers, bicyclists, and horseback riders can enter the carriage-road system from a number of points around the perimeter without passing through the gates, which are used only by park personnel for maintenance-vehicle access. The gate houses, with their whimsical architecture, now serve as a looking-glass transition from the modern automated world into the restful magic beyond.

Wandering along the carriage roads, immersed in nature, the visitor will frequently happen upon rustic stone bridges carefully placed in the landscape by JDR Jr. These handsome architectural elements exemplify the skill of human hands and are reminders of the familiar built world we inhabit, but their design and construction

An early view of the Hemlock Bridge (completed 1924) on the Jordan–Sargent Mountain Road. *C.P. Simpson personal collection*

link them to the past rather than the present. They speak of other times that in our hectic lives we imagine to have been more serene and whole, and they speak of days when there was time to build by hand out of natural materials and when craftsmanship was highly prized. They also connect us to our European roots and our long lineage of design influences. JDR Jr. saw to it that no two bridges were alike; each one was to have its special character as well as a particular view of the landscape.

The stone bridges serve several purposes at Acadia. At the edges of the park, the motor roads pass over or under the carriage roads by means of the bridges, which thus separate the vehicular traffic from the horseback riders, bicyclists, and pedestrians on the carriage roads. Deep in the woods, the bridges span streams or deep ravines, allowing visitors to continue on their way. In visual terms, the bridges form the connections between two parts of the landscape, or two pieces of a road, carrying the eye across stream or ravine and on to the next events. They are also places from which to view the landscape, secure and firm structures offering fine vantage points from which to enjoy particular vistas or rushing streams. Finally, they punctuate the roads as signposts, places to meet or pause for a rest.

The Cobblestone Bridge, which spans Jordan Stream and was the first of the sixteen major bridges built by JDR Jr., fulfills several of these functions. Little viewing turrets built into its parapet encourage travelers to look over the side and down to the woodland stream fringed with mossy rocks and nodding wildflowers. The bridge's structure itself is fascinating, with a long, curving parapet designed to accommodate carriages and with walls constructed entirely of round stones. A footpath runs along the edge of the stream beneath the bridge, allowing scrutiny of the barrel arch's fine stonework.

In addition to the sixteen major stone bridges on the carriage roads, there are any number of very simple smaller bridges that cross little streams. A seventeenth large stone bridge was constructed by the park in 1940 on the Day Mountain carriage road. JDR Jr. loved to lay out his roads so they crossed and recrossed the stream beds, bringing the rider or walker close to the burbling water again and again. In Pocantico, one carriage road has no fewer than sixteen bridges. At Acadia, one section of carriage road that climbs up the north flank of Sargent Mountain is called the Seven Sisters because of the seven little bridges that lie close together along the slope of the hill.

The roadbed itself winds along like a runner of comfort and security in the wild. The materials from which the roads were built are all natural, indigenous to their environment. The creams and light browns of the gravel surface are the same colors as the granite outcroppings on the mountain, so the roads blend well and almost imperceptibly into their surroundings.

Large granite coping stones define the edges of the roads where they skirt the steep mountainsides, providing a light but firm sense of containment and security. Retaining walls, built to support the roadway where it cuts across the mountain face, or to hold back the earth and rock on the uphill side, are so skillfully constructed and so carefully blended into the natural surrounding rock that a casual glance scarcely reveals where one ends and the other begins.

Finally, throughout the system are rustic signposts, placed at intersections, that identify the names of the different road sections and indicate where they lead. The simple cedar posts, with wooden arms and suspended wooden planks, are very much in keeping with the other architectural elements and the scenery. Somehow, the fact that these roads all have names—as do the bridges, mountains, lakes, and streams—adds to the humanness of this landscape, making the wilderness familiar and safe.

Thus, according to JDR Jr.'s meticulous plan, the carriage roads take full advantage of the varied terrain and the unusual combination of features on his beloved Mount Desert. Each section of road has special scenes to recommend it, and the whole system presents a dazzling array of the beauties of the island.

The Building of the Carriage Roads

The formation of Acadia National Park and the building of the carriage-road system was a remarkable odyssey covering more than thirty years, and it commanded the unwavering commitment of its two central figures. Although many others played crucial supporting roles, the park and the carriage roads grew together as the vision of George B. Dorr and JDR Jr. Their persistence carried the process past a great many unforeseen obstacles to result in this natural sanctuary of more than thirty thousand acres with an extensive trail system and fifty-seven miles of carriage roads. Today, Acadia is the second most popular park in the national park system (after Yellowstone). It is the only park in the United States that exists entirely as the result of the generosity of private citizens. All the land in the park was acquired privately and later donated, one-third of it by John D. Rockefeller, Jr.

The creation of the park was an act taken to conserve an extraordinary natural resource, a place of rare beauty. The intention of the early protagonists was to protect the island for its own intrinsic value without altering it in any major way. As we have seen, Dorr became the first public representative of this concept when he took on leadership of the Hancock County Trustees of Public Reservations. Later he became the first park superintendent. JDR Jr.'s contributions included not only his financial support of this organization and the acquisition of thousands of acres of land for the park, but the building of the carriage roads in order to make the park land more accessible.

The transformation from wilderness to park took place in four stages, with some overlap. During the first period, from 1908 until 1914, various private citizens were donating land to the Hancock County Trustees of Public Reservations while JDR Jr. was purchasing land for himself and building his own carriage roads. From 1915 until 1921, JDR Jr. built roads on HCTPR land as well as on his own and also began working in close collaboration with George Dorr. From 1919, when the park was first formed, until 1930, most of the carriage roads were built and JDR Jr.'s land holdings were enlarged considerably. JDR Jr. worked directly with the government as well as with Dorr and continued to build roads simultaneously upon his own land and on park land. Between 1930 and 1940, the carriage-road system was substantially completed. During this period, both the HCTPR and JDR Jr. gradually turned over their lands to the park, including completed carriage roads, so that by 1941 the park was nearly doubled in size. Park attention then shifted to the development of a system of motor roads that JDR Jr. was also deeply involved in building. He remained interested in the park and the carriage roads for the rest of his life, continuing to provide funds for maintenance crews and organizing the cleanup and restoration after the Great Fire of 1947, which devastated the island.

George B. Dorr looking
over his beloved mountains
at Acadia. (From his book,
*Acadia National Park: Its
Origin and Background*,
published 1942.)

Having been introduced through their mutual friend Charles
Eliot, George Dorr and JDR Jr. began a remarkable collaboration.
Each played a crucial role in the development of Acadia National
Park and the carriage roads, and neither could have succeeded
alone. Dorr provided the political skills to complement Rockefeller's
money, mastery of detail, and road-building talents. Yet it was
circumstance and a shared vision that brought them together rather
than natural compatibility. Although both men came from families of
considerable means, they had fundamentally different outlooks.
Dorr was a Boston aristocrat who loved to stalk the wilderness. JDR

Jr. was the son of a self-made man born of farming stock. From his father he learned to care for the land and work with his own hand to display its secret beauty. Dorr was bold and ebullient, and he felt no hesitation about storming bastions in Washington, Boston, or New York. JDR Jr. was an enormously shy and reserved man who preferred to work behind the scenes; he did not enjoy the public role that fortune had thrust upon him.

Dorr's vision was to preserve the "wild and beautiful" lakes, valleys, and mountains of the island as pristine wilderness, modified as little as possible.[7] The extensive trail system that already existed by 1915, laid out by many of the early summer visitors (including himself), represented the extent of human intervention he thought appropriate. He had walked, climbed, and explored every part of the island and knew where to find the remnants of virgin forest, the sheltered valleys with "deep soil and abundant waters" that provided sanctuary for migrating wildlife.[8] He knew the little streams that spawned trout each spring and worked diligently to preserve them. He was a devoted outdoorsman and an amateur naturalist of considerable knowledge.

Dorr was also a highly impulsive man who thought nothing about expending his family's fortune and his own health in service of the growing park. At the end of his long, dedicated life, he had virtually nothing left of his material wealth and was blind—in part because he refused to follow his doctor's orders when they interfered with what he wished to do. Charles Eliot, in a letter responding to JDR Jr.'s queries about how to get information from George Dorr regarding the lands he had put claims on for conservation, spoke plainly about Dorr's virtues and excesses:

> I have been trying for years to induce Mr. Dorr to write down the information he has in his head about lands on the Island which ought to go into either the National Park or the Wild Gardens; but have totally failed in all my efforts to procure that list. He also has much lore about the plant and animal life on Mount Desert, and about its history, which ought to have been written down years ago; but he has on paper only scattered memoranda that nobody else could make anything out of, and he himself cannot find when he wants them. I fear that the situation is a hopeless one. Furthermore, Dorr lives in such a preposterous way as respects the care of his health, and takes so many absurd risks in rushing about this Island that we are likely to lose him any day by disease or accident.[9]

Despite his wild ways (which included frequent plunges into the frigid North Atlantic) and Eliot's predictions, George Dorr lived to the advanced age of ninety-four, never ceasing for a moment in the pursuit of his visions for Acadia National Park.

JDR Jr. was no less devoted to Mount Desert Island, but his focus and style were very different. Even though he was also a conservationist who believed strongly in the benefits of time spent out-of-doors and in the importance of safeguarding nature, he sought a balance between preservation and access. In Laurance Rockefeller's words, "He wished the land to be preserved but not hidden; he wanted it to be revealed to the people."[10] JDR Jr. understood well that carriage roads winding through the forests and along the mountainsides would offer the benefits and beauties of nature to all who would come to explore the island.

In his methods of working and living, JDR Jr. was very much Dorr's antithesis. He carefully planned every move, never doing anything he had not thoroughly investigated first and keeping everything in order at all times. Freeman Tilden, a prominent park historian, related a wonderfully revealing story that he says used to be told in Acadia:

> . . . Mr. Rockefeller gave George Dorr a friendly suggestion as to the evils of dilatoriness and procrastination.
>
> "Why, I myself," he said, "check my affairs every night before I go to bed."
>
> George Dorr looked a little saddened, like an erring child corrected by a kind parent. Then he suggested, hopefully, "Wouldn't once a week be often enough?"[11]

JDR Jr., deeply disturbed by Dorr's reckless expenditure of his personal resources, confided to a superintendent at Mesa Verde National Park that a dear friend of his was reducing his assets precariously in attempts to extend Acadia's park area, despite the admonitions and opposition of all his conservative friends.[12] In fact, as early as 1915, Dorr was unable to help with the purchase of lands that were essential for the boundaries of the Sieur de Monts National Monument because "he had already put more money into this enterprise on behalf of the public than he should have done; and . . . his estate was seriously embarrassed in consequence."[13] On at least one occasion, JDR Jr. and Charles Eliot rescued Dorr from some of the debts he had incurred in pursuit of his vision, and on other occasions JDR Jr. purchased lands Dorr had acquired earlier, giving them to the park.

As has been intimated, JDR Jr. was very much an expert in road building and Dorr decidedly was not. This did not in the least deter George Dorr from feeling free to advise JDR Jr.'s contractors on the alignment of roads being built within the park or to make suggestions regarding other road-building details. His interference not only irritated the contractors but also caused tension between the two men. But, having joined forces, the two were held on course by their common love of the land, and in spite of their differences, they worked together for more than twenty years with mutual respect, with forbearance when they disagreed, and without significant difficulty.

In characteristic fashion, JDR Jr. proceeded to plan and build his roads in an orderly manner. At the same time as he was renovating and expanding his newly acquired cottage on Barr Hill, he built carriage roads around his house, down to his stable, and on around the edge of Long Pond, where he also constructed a small boathouse with a charming veranda. These first roads allowed him to pass through the moss- and fern-filled woods high up in his domain, so he could enjoy glimpses of the sea and the mountains. Or he could drive down in the evening light to Long Pond, where the great blue heron still spreads its silent wings in the dusk.

JDR Jr. and Abby always loved to walk or ride on the roads and paths he built. Late-afternoon drives were a special favorite. Even after their children were grown and had families, they still enjoyed those drives. On one occasion, as they passed near the house of one of their sons, at the base of Barr Hill, they encountered two of their small grandchildren. Apparently the two had decided to run away and were on their way up the hill and into the woods, each carrying a remnant of dinner for provisions. The grandparents engaged the children in conversation, and after ascertaining their mission, managed to gently persuade them to reconsider—at least for the time being.

By 1911, once the work around his estate was underway, JDR Jr. began purchasing additional large tracts of land to the northwest of Barr Hill extending all the way to Jordan Pond, in an area with a lovely, meandering woodland stream. Westward of Long Pond, he bought land up on a hill with views out over the Western Way. He began to lay out roads there and contemplated connecting all of them to each other and to the roads around Barr Hill. To do so, he needed to cross over a section of land that belonged to the Reservation (as the HCTPR lands were called), and he asked George Dorr how this might be done. At the time, Dorr was in the midst of trying to secure government acceptance of the Reservation lands under the National Monument Act. He and the other trustees, while interested in having the carriage roads built, wanted to be sure not to jeopardize their cause with the government or the future right of public access.

Finally it was worked out that JDR Jr. could build the carriage

Family photos around The Eyrie: Young David rides with his parents in the canopy-top surrey, 1917; JDR Jr. with Winthrop, 1915; Abby with Laurance and Winthrop, 1915.
Rockefeller Archive Center

JDR Jr. and Abby at The Eyrie, 1915. *Rockefeller Archive Center*

roads but he would have no permanent easements or other legal rights to the land. This arrangement was acceptable to him, and in September of 1915 the HCTPR passed a resolution giving him permission to construct the roads. So began the cooperation between JDR Jr. and the Trustees. He extended his roads across the Reservation property at his own expense, as he was to do in the future.

At the same time, JDR Jr. also purchased farmland on the western shore of Long Pond, securing a beautiful field with old apple trees overlooking the water, as well as the hill beyond. To connect this property to the earlier purchase on the opposite side of the pond, he needed to cross over at the southern end, right next to the public road. The pond extends almost to the town road at that point, and the ocean presses in closely on the other side, allowing no leeway to conceal the carriage crossing. After this Long Pond Crossing, as JDR Jr. referred to it, had been staked out at approximately the same level as the existing road, his close friend Charles Eliot apparently had some words with him about its location, resulting in these suggestions from Eliot:

What I was anxious for was that no higher road built by you across the southerly end of Long Pond should impair the beauty of the view up the Pond towards the hills, which the passer-by now gets from the public highway—the most beautiful view on the Island. That the State and not you would own the new road would not diminish my anxiety at all. You would have done the harm—all the same.

If you need a private road at that spot to connect your roads on the east side of the Pond with your roads on the west side, why not lower somewhat your present stakes, and then build up the highway; so that passers-by can look over the side-walls of your road, and so lose only a few rods of the Pond?[14]

A 1932 Alfred Mullikin photograph of Long Pond from the carriage road crossing. Charles Eliot considered this "the most beautiful view on the Island." *Rockefeller Archive Center.*

The Long Pond Crossing is indeed quite a bit lower than the motor road, indicating that JDR Jr. must have taken Eliot's suggestions to heart, in spite of what must have been considerable additional expense. In this way, the original view up the graceful little pond is not only preserved but also enhanced by the elevation of the town road above the level of the pond. The carriage road, nearly at pond level, is very unobtrusive. Such receptiveness to the suggestions and opinions of others was not unusual for JDR Jr. He always took pains to listen to thoughtful comment from peers and workers alike, and when he was persuaded of the merits of a proposal, he had no qualms about acting on it.

Eliot concluded his letter with a comment about one of the new carriage roads west of Long Pond, expressing the friendship and admiration that existed between the two men and Eliot's firm support of JDR Jr.'s roads: "Mrs. Eliot and I lately walked slowly over your new road—your most westerly road—and found it altogether admirable. I suppose that you appreciate the fact that well-built roads are the most durable works of man. They outlast all other structures and monuments."[15]

During this first period of road building, JDR Jr. established the methods of operation that he was to use, with few variations, over the succeeding years. He first found capable people to work with him and then utilized their services fully, while never relinquishing leadership of the work or his personal attention to details. In matters of land acquisition, he always preferred to investigate the availability of properties through a third party, as quietly as possible, in order to avoid unduly inflating land values or stirring up controversy. He continued to use the services of Albert H. Lynam in Bar Harbor and also worked with George Stebbins of Cooksey Realty Company in Seal Harbor. As a devoted early summer resident of Seal Harbor, Stebbins knew the available lands in that area extremely well. He also had been responsible for laying out the roads and land plots on the eastern side of Seal Harbor, where the first summer homes were built before JDR Jr.'s arrival.

After building the first roads using only a contractor, JDR Jr. was most fortunate in discovering Charles P. Simpson, an engineer from the mainland town of Sullivan. Simpson was already sixty-seven when he started to work for Rockefeller in 1916. He had had no formal education, but as a young man he had traveled West in search of work, apprenticed to a cousin in California who was an engineer, and become very skillful at his profession. His projects included work for

Charles P. Simpson, shown here during the 1920s, was the first engineer hired by JDR Jr. to work on the carriage roads. *C.P. Simpson personal collection*

The gracefully curved Amphitheater Bridge, completed 1931, is on the Amphitheater section of the Asticou–Jordan Pond carriage road. *Mary Louise Pierson photo*

Looking west across Eagle Lake toward Cadillac Mountain from the Eagle Lake carriage road.
Mary Louise Pierson photo

Rustic signposts guide travelers through Mount Desert's elaborate network of carriage roads. *Mary Louise Pierson photo*

Little Harbor Brook Bridge, on the Gardner–Mitchell Hill carriage road, was completed in 1919. *Mary Louise Pierson photo*

Some portions of the carriage roads bring travelers to panoramic outlooks, while others offer intimate woodland views. This peaceful stretch is on the east side of Eagle Lake. *Ann R. Roberts photo*

Completed in 1932, the Brown Mountain gate house is on the Upper Hadlock Pond Road. Both it and the Jordan Pond Gate House were designed in a style typical of traditional French architecture. *Mary Louise Pierson photo*

Looking west across the pond from the Mountain motor road, one can see where the Jordan–Sargent Mountain carriage road crosses the Jordan Pond rock slide. *Mary Louise Pierson photo*

West Branch Bridge, completed in 1931, is one of three on the Asticou–Jordan Pond carriage road.
Mary Louise Pierson photo

Cliffside Bridge, also on the Asticou–Jordan Pond carriage road, was completed in 1932.
Mary Louise Pierson photo

Drainage was given careful attention in the road designs, and culverts were artfully constructed of hand-cut stones. *Mary Louise Pierson photo*

"Where the road turns around the top of the bluff and the view to the Northeast over the bay is magnificent, only low material should be used such as the low honeysucle, blackberries, asters, wild roses, etc." noted Mrs. Farrand as she and JDR Jr. planned roadside plantings for the Paradise Hill loop. *Mary Louise Pierson photo*

Two elements of Rockefeller's carriage roads—coping stones and skillfully integrated retaining walls—can be seen on the Day Mountain loop. *Mary Louise Pierson photo*

landscape architect Joseph Curtis in Northeast Harbor, work for the town of Northeast Harbor, laying out the Kebo Valley Golf Club in Bar Harbor, and laying out the railroad line between Ellsworth and Machias. Each day he took the boat across Frenchman Bay from Sullivan to Mount Desert to work for JDR Jr.; he laid out all the carriage roads from 1916 to 1922, when he retired because of poor health.

His grandson and namesake (known as Chip) recalls the deep friendship and respect between his grandfather and JDR Jr. He also tells a delightful story of a visit that JDR Jr. and Abby made to the Simpsons at their home in Sullivan. When it was time to leave, Abby went upstairs to refresh herself before the homeward journey. When she did not reappear, they found her accidentally locked in the bathroom, and none of them, despite their best efforts, could get the door open. Finally they had to go out onto the roof of the house and rescue her through the bathroom window. The Simpsons were most impressed by the calm and good humor displayed by both Rockefellers throughout this adventure.[16]

After Charles Simpson's retirement, his son, Paul D. Simpson, worked for JDR Jr. as chief engineer until 1940, when the carriage roads were complete. After that, he continued as an engineering consultant to Rockefeller until the mid-1950s. His formal training and experience, in addition to exposure to his father's sensitive eye and skillful hand, prepared him well for his work with JDR Jr. After

Paul D. Simpson became carriage-road engineer after his father's retirement in 1922. He is shown here with son Chip in 1933. *C.P. Simpson personal collection*

Paul Simpson and family take an outing on the carriage roads in the early 1930s. Mr. Peyton, from the Jordan Pond Stables, is on the far left. *C.P. Simpson personal collection*

obtaining a civil engineering degree from the University of Maine, Paul headed west as his father had done and worked on engineering projects for the Bureau of Land Reclamation until the elder Simpson became ill. Paul returned as a seasoned engineer confident in his abilities and ready to assume the consuming task of laying out the bulk of the carriage-road system under the exacting eye of JDR Jr. Chip Simpson remembers JDR Jr.'s grave formality when he arrived in Maine and called to tell Paul that he would pick him up to ride the carriage roads. He also recalls his father's long hours at work—until midnight or later, and beginning again at five-thirty in the morning. Even then, Paul sometimes brought plans home for further study so he would be ready for JDR Jr.'s queries. Since childhood, Paul had known JDR Jr., having watched him on the carriage roads as he pulled red flagging out of his pocket to mark trees to be cut, always insisting on saving as many as possible. He also remembered, when working as a young bellhop at the Seaside Inn, JDR Jr.'s appreciation when he served his meals.[17]

The third engineer who worked on the carriage roads was Walters G. Hill, of Bar Harbor. Hill also came from an engineering family, and his father had worked on many of Bar Harbor's town roads. Walters Hill worked closely with Paul Simpson on the later carriage roads and the motor roads, and, like Paul Simpson, he held the work and JDR Jr. in high regard. His daughter, Irene Hill Marinke, remembers riding around the Witch Hole and Paradise Hill carriage roads with her father to inspect the work. She recalls the meticulousness of his work and how he carried every detail of the road layout in his head. He even knew the exact grade of any segment of road. He was a hands-on man, working out of the back of his car and a small house behind their home. Hill's devotion to JDR Jr. grew out of Rockefeller's consideration for the men who worked for him—he never failed to inquire about them on a personal note. Hill also did the survey of the Cadillac Mountain motor road for JDR Jr. and worked on the Ocean Drive and Stanley Brook motor roads.[18]

Early on, JDR Jr. established his own engineering office in Seal Harbor, and all the work was directed out of that office. The actual building of the roads and bridges was done by various local contractors and stonemasons. The first (and most prominent) contractors were Alanson E. Clement and Chauncey D. Joy. The high quality of their work ensured that they would continue to build roads for Rockefeller for many years. In addition, there were the contractor Byron W. Candage and his son Samuel Candage, a stonemason, both of whom worked skillfully on the bridges as well as the carriage roads. Charles Miller, a local nurseryman, worked with JDR Jr. to clean up and plant the roadsides as well as to do forestry work. Over

Members of the Duck Brook Bridge road crew, 1924. At that time, common laborers earned $3.50 a day, and stonecutters $6.00. *Bar Harbor Times*

the years, other contractors and stonemasons were involved, as well as large road crews of up to thirty men at a time. During the late 1920s and the 1930s, Rockefeller, ever attentive to cost, used his superintendent, S.F. Ralston, as contractor and hired his own road crews for some of the carriage-road construction.

JDR Jr. established the initial line that a road was to follow by studying maps of the areas and walking or riding extensively in the field. Charles Simpson, and later Paul, did the surveys and the calculations for grades, and they made suggestions for how the alignment could be improved. Then JDR Jr. responded with his own comments. During the times when JDR Jr. was in Maine, he spent a great deal of time walking or riding with Simpson and the contractors to be sure their plans were just right. In between, they carried on an extensive correspondence about each segment of road, making proposals back and forth, exchanging sketches, checking to be sure the grades and turnings were comfortable for carriages, and keeping an eye out for beautiful views. In a 1918 letter to George Dorr, JDR Jr. described this process:

> I have been working on the survey of these new roads for some time and spent a few days at Seal Harbor late in November going over them finally with Mr. Simpson. I feel sure that they are rightly located, for the entire section both north and south of the Asticou Jordan Pond trail was carefully and repeatedly cruised, first by Mr. Simpson and then by me, before these locations were decided upon.

In the same letter, JDR Jr. spoke very persuasively of why he was interested in a particular route:

> The purpose of this letter is to ask if the Trustees, or if you, as Curator of the Reservation, will give me authority to build this additional road. . . . [T]his road is not necessary as a part of the above described scheme but it develops very beautiful country, passing over the top of Bear Hill

traversed by no paths from which a really marvellous view of the sea as well as of the mountains is obtained, and runs up Little Harbor brook as far as a reasonable grade will permit, crossing the brook from time to time.

He then went on to discuss how this road fitted in with another one he was requesting permission to build at the same time:

Although these two new roads which I am now asking permission to build seem quite close to each other on the map, in reality they are not visible . . . one from the other except at one or two points, and they develop quite different country, all of which is exceptionally beautiful and very little used or known at present.

And finally, he spoke about how he was planning each segment of road in relation to the larger whole:

Following this plan of operation will permit the extension of the system little by little, making each portion available and complete in itself and giving time to do the work in an economical and orderly manner.[19]

Meanwhile, the Northeast Harbor Village Improvement Society was busy building its own bridle paths in the area around Lower and Upper Hadlock ponds. Their Bridle Path Committee, established in 1915 in the wake of the arrival of automobiles, specifically intended to connect their horse paths with Rockefeller's carriage roads. During this early time, they were clearly enthusiastic about what Rockefeller was doing, since they perceived his roads as a happy extension of their own. In fact, following their unsuccessful attempts to raise funds for a bridle path connecting to his Mitchell Hill horse road, JDR Jr. stepped in and incorporated the road into his system, building it as a full carriage road at his own expense.

After the initial five thousand acres had been designated the Sieur de Monts National Monument in 1916 by President Wilson, George Dorr worked hard to gather the support of the local summer people for the Hancock County Trustees of Public Reservations in order to continue purchasing strategic pieces of land. In the meantime, JDR Jr. saw that the original HCTPR holdings were composed largely of mountaintops with very few connections, so he began to buy the surrounding lands to ensure that the proposed park would comprise a unified piece that included both mountains and valleys.[20] He studied the entire eastern half of the island with an exacting eye, and he planned where the roads might go to show the delights of the area to the best advantage. He then purchased the necessary acreage to make the connections.

George Dorr was intent on facilitating communications be-

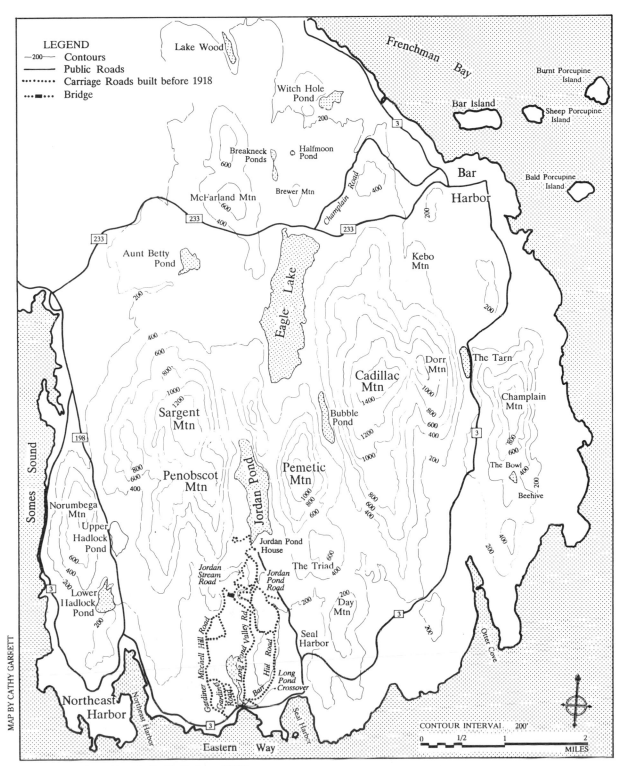

LEGEND
—200— Contours
——— Public Roads
•••••• Carriage Roads built before 1918
•••■•••• Bridge

Lake Wood

Frenchman Bay

Witch Hole Pond

Burnt Porcupine Island

Bar Island

Sheep Porcupine Island

Breakneck Ponds

Halfmoon Pond

600

Bald Porcupine Island

McFarland Mtn

Brewer Mtn

600

Bar Harbor

400

200

Kebo Mtn

233

400

233

233

Aunt Betty Pond

200

200

Eagle Lake

Dorr Mtn

The Tarn

Champlain Mtn

400

600

Cadillac Mtn

1000

800

1200

1400

1000

800

600

400

3

800

600

Sargent Mtn

Bubble Pond

1200

200

Somes Sound

800

600

400

Penobscot Mtn

Jordan Pond

Pemetic Mtn

1000

800

400

The Bowl

400

200

Beehive

198

1000

800

600

400

200

Norumbega Mtn

Upper Hadlock Pond

600

400

200

Jordan Pond House

Jordan Stream Road

Jordan Pond Road

The Triad

600

400

200

Lower Hadlock Pond

3

200

Day Mtn

3

200

Otter Cove

200

Gardiner Mitchell Hill Road

Gardiner Road

Long Pond Valley Rd.

Barr Hill Road

Seal Harbor

200

Long Pond Crossover

Northeast Harbor

Northeast Harbor

Seal Harbor

Eastern Way

3

CONTOUR INTERVAL 200'

0   1/2   1   2
MILES

MAP BY CATHY GARRETT

Map 5: Carriage Roads Built Before 1918

tween Rockefeller and the newly formed National Park Service. He negotiated with Secretary of the Interior Franklin Lane for the authority Rockefeller needed to build on government land. He also persuaded Lane to pay a visit to Acadia in 1917 to see the new national monument created the year before. During this visit, Dorr arranged for JDR Jr. to invite Secretary Lane to luncheon at The Eyrie. JDR Jr. presented his latest plans for an extended road system to be built at his own expense, some on his land and some on government property. Secretary Lane immediately gave his verbal permission for these plans, and the agreement was confirmed by the government early in the following year. In addition, Dorr secured Lane's promise for a government regulation barring automobiles from the carriage roads. He wrote to JDR Jr.:

> Secretary Lane has given me power to meet you fully in the matter [of issuing permission to build carriage roads on government lands] and has besides authorized me at my request to close to motor use, in the Park Service name, the roads you build within the park. This is far better than to have exclusion depend solely on your control of entrance, and gives you the support of the Government in making the system motor free, which may save complications in the future.
>
> ...I should only like to have you consult with me about your plans from time to time, as opportunity comes, and to be made conversant with them in advance so far as possible. You know that area in a way that I do not, and I shall rely on your good judgement regarding it and its development in the public interest. It is a superb opportunity in a landscape sense; I know of nothing like it in the East, and what is done will be at once enduring and singularly conspicuous.[21]

Thus, the burden of safeguarding the carriage roads from motor vehicles was upon the Park Service rather than on JDR Jr.'s shoulders. In his reply, he was thankful for Dorr's action and appreciative of his support:

> I appreciate your forethought in regard to my possible plans and desires in the matter of roads and also the complete confidence which you repose in me in the matter of working out these plans. You know that whatever is done will be done with the same painstaking care, forethought and study that I would put into work on my own property, and more no man can do. . . .
>
> Your idea of securing Secretary Lane's authorization to close to automobiles those portions of roads which I have already built through the Government property thus relieving me from being the sole obstacle to such use of the roads, is an excellent one and greatly appreciated.
>
> Again I thank you for the complete sympathy and cooperation which you have given me in the development of this road system and for the authority to proceed with the work according to my best judgement.[22]

As JDR Jr. built one road after another, he gradually opened up more of the area between his property around Long Pond and the rather different tracts near Northeast Harbor and Jordan Pond—all according to his plan. Between 1917 and 1920, he also built three rustic stone bridges, the first of the sixteen that became part of the system. He was in full stride and just preparing to begin construction on the Amphitheater Road, the last of the roads authorized by Secretary Lane, when opposition to his work erupted in the summer of 1920.

CHAPTER 4

Perseverance Amid Controversy

The route of the Amphitheater Road proposed by John D. Rockefeller, Jr., penetrated an especially wild and beautiful valley that cut in deeply between Cedar Swamp and Sargent mountains and was accessible only by footpaths. On August 15, 1920, JDR Jr. received a handwritten letter from George Wharton Pepper, a longtime summer resident of Northeast Harbor, commending him for the completed roads, but asking that he build no more in this particular valley. He wrote:

> I trust that plans for extending a road through the Amphitheatre have not been carried beyond the point at which reconsideration is possible. In my judgement it would be a serious mistake to extend yr well-conceived system of roads into this area. The peculiar charm of this island consists in a happy combination of untouched natural beauty and such a development of means of communication as is incidental to our delightful social life. This means Wilderness and Park—isolation and accessibility. . . . the Amphitheatre, is an as yet unbroken forest—a wilderness of tree-tops. Pierce this with a road or roads and its character will vanish. Not merely will its beauty be marred when viewed from the heights, but the sense of remoteness which now gives it charm will be replaced by the realization of accessibility. This means that the Park will be overdeveloped and due proportion of Wilderness destroyed.
> . . . If the Amphitheatre is pierced my own interest in the Eastern part of the island will to a great extent evaporate. I have loved the place for thirty years. There are many many lovers of the Island and admirers of yours who feel as I do.[1]

Suddenly, as the magnitude of what JDR Jr. was doing began to be apparent to the summer folk of Northeast Harbor, their enthusiasm turned to distress. Pepper, a prominent lawyer and social activist from Philadelphia, represented in his views the feelings of many of the earliest summer families to settle on the island. The conflict echoed the differences between George Dorr and JDR Jr. It was essentially a very old controversy, one that has divided the conservation movement from the beginning.

On one side were those who believed that wilderness areas

Opposite: **Engineer's stakes mark the difficult route where the Jordan–Sargent Mountain carriage road crosses the rock slide.** *C.P. Simpson personal collection*

should be left as wild as possible and that human interference should be minimal. Many of the summer residents of Northeast Harbor had been visiting the island for years and exploring its pristine and remote interior on foot, knowing all the little springs, the bogs where orchids grew, and the views from each peak. The extensive network of footpaths that they had built allowed them to slip through the woods and ascend the peaks with minimal impact. In their minds, that was the only intrusion necessary to give access to the wild interior regions of the place. They felt access should be reserved for those who were willing to make the effort. In this way, the most fragile and remote areas would be protected from the casual and possibly destructive masses.

On the other side were those like JDR Jr., who felt that the inner regions of the island were so beautiful that they should be made accessible. Representing the view that the hand of humans could improve nature, and that proper intervention would aid preservation, he believed that his roads would ultimately enhance rather than destroy the landscape.

Neither side was about to change its beliefs, but JDR Jr. had no desire to alienate the community, so he halted construction at once on the Amphitheater Road in deference to the concerns articulated by Pepper and others. With his characteristic thoroughness, diplomacy, and restraint, he stated his position clearly in his reply to Pepper:

> Until the receipt of your letter of August 15th I had assumed that the roads built during the last few years through our place and made available for horse and pedestrian travel to our neighbors on the island, as well as those which extend into the National Park were favorably regarded and entirely approved by the people on the island generally.
>
> It is hardly necessary for me to say that in so far as the roads extending into the National Park are concerned, I have taken no action which was not at the outset carefully considered and duly authorized. . . .
>
> The continuation of the Brown Mountain–Jordan Pond roads, upon which work was recently begun, is a part of the general scheme which was worked out at the very outset, and towards the completion of which the various pieces built up to date have contributed.
>
> Since the receipt of your letter I have held up for the time being all work on the road, for irrespective of the official authorization under which I have been proceeding, I would be unwilling to continue any portion of the work, if after the whole scheme is understood there would be instead of cordial approval any considerable intelligent opposition to it on the part of those interested. . . .
>
> May I say in closing that I appreciate the frankness of your note and shall value the opportunity of exchanging views with you in regard to this whole matter at such time and in such way as you may name.[2]

JDR Jr. offered at once to meet with Pepper and representatives of the village improvement societies to go over the route of the proposed road. Each society sent a delegation, and a small party, including George Pepper and George Dorr, walked over the proposed line with JDR Jr. on two different occasions.

After these excursions, JDR Jr. wrote an eloquent letter to Lincoln Cromwell, president of the Northeast Harbor Village Improvement Society, expressing his sentiments about this piece of road and talking about his own road-building experience:

> Because I was brought up in the woods I have always loved the trees, the rocks, the hills and the valleys. For over five years I have been studying and preparing for the construction of the road under discussion, with every inch of which I am familiar, and had thought that by building it, it would be possible, without interfering with the enjoyment of those who are able to walk the trails, to make available, views of unsurpassed beauty and sections otherwise inaccessible, to the many who could not reach them except with horses, as well as to that also large number of people who find walking on roads more comfortable than the rougher and steeper trails.
>
> Because I have built paths and roads almost since childhood and know how quickly nature obliterates the scars necessarily made at the outset, I have realized as perhaps few others have, that the conspicuousness of some of the newer roads would soon disappear and they would almost become obliterated as has the Barr Hill Road, one of the first built. . . .[3]

At the end of the letter, he reiterated his intention to discontinue construction in spite of the fact that he felt those "apprehensive that their [the proposed roads'] newness will be permanent, will themselves come to see that the extension of the system as originally planned will mean only temporary conspicuousness." He sent a copy of this letter to George Pepper as a courtesy and received by return mail a remarkable reply in which Pepper rejoiced in Rockefeller's decision to halt construction and wrestled with the philosophical dilemma posed by the roads. He wrote:

> Early this morning I went alone up the ridges of Sargent Mt and sat for an hour or so at the point where our view of the Amphitheatre was the other day obscured by fog. The wind was doing whimsical things with the clouds; and shadow and sunlight were chasing each other over the tree-tops. There was not, as far as I could see, a living creature on either ridge and no sign of man's existence except distant sails and almost indistinguishable buildings on the far-away islands. The mountains and the valley which they enshrine seemed to stand as untouched bits of God's handiwork. As I sat there I reviewed the situation about which we have been in conference. I came to the conclusion that the question between us is one of those matters of original apprehension of which it cannot be

affirmed that either side is right or either side is wrong. If the untouched Amphitheatre is worth preserving for those who can conquer its defenses, then the road should not be built. If the road would not mar the Amphitheatre—or if, even if marred, the valley should be made accessible to those who cannot climb—then the road ought to be built. And there you are! —I came back to the house with these thoughts in mind and found yr friendly letter enclosing a copy of communication to Mr. Cromwell. I learned with intense satisfaction of yr magnanimous decision to postpone for the present the building of the Amphitheatre Road and to halt the road from the Jordan Stream bridge at the point where, among the poplars, the Jordan ledge commands a wonderful view of the sea and shore. I sat down at once to write you this letter of high appreciation.[4]

Subsequently, the Northeast Harbor and Seal Harbor village improvement societies held special meetings to vote on the matter. In Seal Harbor, two resolutions were proposed, each one strongly defended, and although the resolution in favor of Rockefeller continuing his road construction won, it was only by one vote. In Northeast Harbor, on the other hand, the meeting was reported to have had the largest attendance ever recorded, and the group voted unanimously to endorse the continuation of the proposed carriage road. It is interesting to note that Pepper was not notified of this meeting until afterward, when Lincoln Cromwell called to inform him of the vote! Those many summer residents in favor of the "Rockefeller Roads" were making themselves known.

The report made to the Seal Harbor Village Improvement Society by a Mr. Montague (one of the members) before their special meeting strongly presented the views of those in favor of the Amphitheater Road and also clarified some of the opposition's fears. It says, in part:

If number and continuity and beauty of views be the test, the proposed road will excel any of the trails looking down upon the Amphitheatre. If the greatest good to the greatest number be the test, the proposed road, by opening all these views to those dependent on roads and horses, as well as to walkers, will give opportunities for pleasure to many more visitors than do or can use any of the trails. Against all this it is objected, however, that no matter how laid out or constructed, the proposed road will be visible in several places, from occasional points in the trails around the Amphitheatre, and to that extent it will break in upon the sweeping wilderness view now obtained from various points along these trails, and that therefore no road of any kind should be built in or around the Amphitheatre, or in that large area of the National Park lying between Sargent Mountain and Asticou. How fallacious is this . . . assumption that the proposed road will necessarily leave ugly permanent scars. Nature, with her weathering and her green growth, had rapidly reclaimed the cutting, the margins, and even the roadbed, of Mr. Rockefeller's older roads, as everyone knows who is familiar with his Barr Hill Road, and Nature may be called upon to do the same in the proposed Amphitheatre Road. That the beauties of the Amphitheatre and the sweeping sea and island views it commands, which now are in large part invisible from any trail, but which Mr. Rockefeller's generosity, perseverance and skill would now open to all who can ride or walk, should be permanently locked against all who are dependent on roads and horses, and kept as the exclusive possession of those only who can climb trails, and to them visible only from occasional points, and in many instances not visible from any, is a proposal which cannot be justified. Such will be the result, however, if the objection to the proposed road prevails. Officials of other National and State Parks and the permanent residents and summer visitors who have used these roads regard them as one of the chief delights of Mt. Desert. This report seems an appropriate occasion for recording this society's gratitude for Mr. Rockefeller's system of existing roads, as well as its approval of his proposed Amphitheatre Road.[5]

George Dorr was also very much involved in the discussions. Rockefeller had notified him at once on receipt of Pepper's first letter, and he was very concerned about safeguarding the interests of the park. As park superintendent and therefore the government representative, he was invited to attend the meeting of the Northeast Harbor Village Improvement Society. When he could not be present, he sent a long letter assuring them of his support for the Amphitheater Road, reiterating its full authorization by himself and the government, and giving his answers to the fears engendered. He assured them that the proposed carriage road would not penetrate deep into the wilds at the head of the Amphitheater; he spoke of how valuable this road would be as a fire guard as well as an opportunity for riders. He also argued that the road scars would be quickly obliterated, as "Nature is exceedingly prolific in this region, clothing even the most barren spots with vegetation. . . ," and the roadbed itself would be obscured by overhanging trees. At the end of the letter, he wrote of his own feelings on the matter and proposed a way to elicit positive support:

> Personally, I feel so strongly that it would be a misfortune [if] work so well conceived and carried out till now should be interrupted at its present stage by adverse criticism, and so convinced that that criticism has been founded mainly upon misconceptions which further study or fuller statement would eliminate, that I offer, should you deem it desirable, to join with others in signing—and as the Government's representative to head—a request to Mr. Rockefeller to continue the road construction planned, authorized by Secretary Lane. This would serve as a means of bringing out the sentiment of the people interested pro and con and show if I am right in thinking the weight of public opinion to be strongly in favor of the road's continuance.[6]

Meanwhile, knowledge of the controversy was filtering into the community. Other private citizens began writing to JDR Jr. in support of his work. One man wrote that as far as he was concerned, "successful opposition to the enlargement of this system of roads would be in the nature of a public misfortune." Petitions began circulating, and records show 168 names requesting that JDR Jr. "reconsider and complete the road as planned"; forty-three names appeared on a petition expressing "profound satisfaction with his decision to postpone for the present the further extension of that system in the Sargent–Jordan Amphitheatre," while at the same time assuring him of their "appreciation of the intelligence and generosity with which he is developing his system of roads."[7]

Then, on September 8, 1920, the *Bar Harbor Times* published a major article and an editorial on the subject. It included lengthy quotes from Rockefeller's letters to George Pepper and Lincoln Cromwell and sections of Montague's report to the Seal Harbor Village Improvement Society. The paper came out in full support of the new carriage road and the road work in general, citing the great value of the carriage roads to the community and the wide public approval for Rockefeller's efforts among both summer and winter residents.[8]

All of this outpouring of support caused JDR Jr. to reevaluate the situation carefully but not to change his position or take any new action. In his cautious manner, he gathered information from both sides, even asking George Pepper to supply him with a list of names of those who were opposed to the construction so that he could gauge their number and hear their concerns.

Finally, on September 16, JDR Jr. wrote again to George Pepper, including excerpts from a letter he had written to two other nervous summer residents in an attempt to allay their fears about building over the mountaintops and allowing cars on the carriage roads. This letter revealed his firm intention to preserve the mountaintops from development and keep cars off the carriage roads, despite the growing number of visitors and automobiles.

I fancy that people generally are under a misapprehension as regards what has been called my "scheme of road building." I would be as opposed as anyone could be to the construction of roads on the top of Jordan or Sargent Mountain, and I would not have been interested to build any roads had I thought they would ever be made available for automobiles.

Road building through rocky ledges is expensive. Moreover, such roads continuing any distance above timber line are not interesting or desirable except for the view thus obtained. With the complete view of the island which the top of Green Mountain [now called Cadillac Moun-

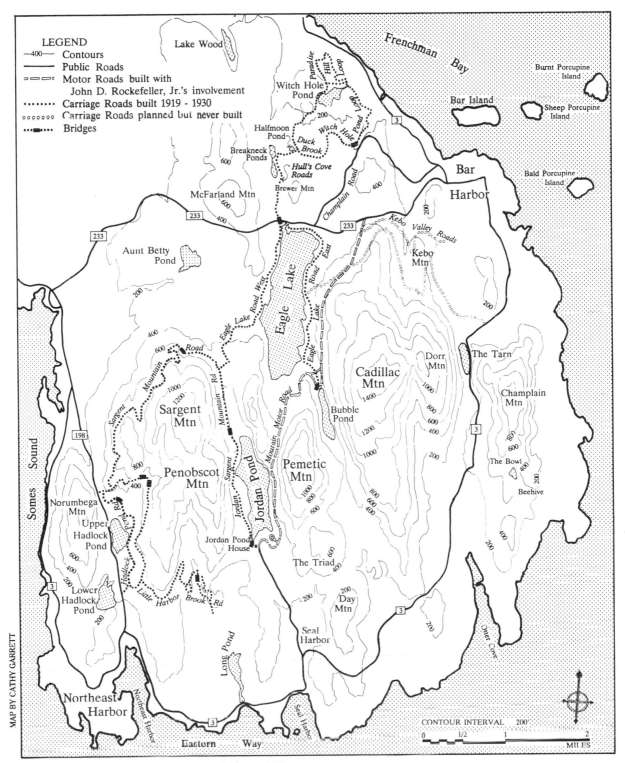

LEGEND

—400— Contours
——— Public Roads
▭ ▭ ▭ ▭ Motor Roads built with
     John D. Rockefeller, Jr.'s involvement
•••••••• Carriage Roads built 1919 - 1930
ooooooo Carriage Roads planned but never built
••■•••• Bridges

Lake Wood

Frenchman Bay

Burnt Porcupine Island

Paradise Hill Loop

Witch Hole Pond

door

Witch Hole Pond

Bar Island

Sheep Porcupine Island

Halfmoon Pond

Duck Brook

Hull's Cove Roads

Breakneck Ponds

600

McFarland Mtn

600

Brewer Mtn

Champlain Road

400

Bar Harbor

Bald Porcupine Island

233

400

233

Aunt Betty Pond

233

Kebo Valley Roads

Kebo Mtn

200

200

200

Eagle Lake Road West

Eagle Lake

Eagle Lake Road East

Mountain Rd

400

Road

600

1000

Sargent Mountain

1200

Sargent Mtn

Dorr Mtn

The Tarn

Cadillac Mtn

1400

1000

Champlain Mtn

800

600

400

200

Bubble Pond

1200

1000

The Bowl

800

600

400

Beehive

200

198

Penobscot Mtn

800

Sargent

400

Jordan Pond

Mountain Motor Road

Pemetic Mtn

1000

800

600

200

Norumbega Mtn

Hadlock

Upper Hadlock Pond

Jordan

Jordan Pond House

The Triad

800

600

400

3

3

600

400

Lower Hadlock Pond

200

Little Harbor Brook Rd

200

The Triad

600

400

350

Day Mtn

200

Somes Sound

Long Pond

Seal Harbor

200

200

Northeast Harbor

Northeast Harbor

Seal Harbor

3

Otter Cove

Eastern Way

CONTOUR INTERVAL   200'

0   1/2   1   2
MILES

MAP BY CATHY GARRETT

Map 6: Carriage Roads Built from 1919 to 1930

tain] gives, and with the extra-ordinarily beautiful views which can be obtained from the carriage roads constructed below the summit of some of the other mountains, where they would be largely through the woods, emerging for views only at intervals, I can see no possible reasons that could be advanced with any force whatever for the construction of a road to the top of any other mountain.[9]

He concluded by saying, "This letter requires no acknowledgment, and I promise you it is my 'Swan Song.'" This letter effectively marked the end of the debate, and although JDR Jr. continued to discuss the matter, he maintained his earlier decision not to renew construction in the Amphitheater area for the time being. The only exception was a small section of road running south from the Jordan Pond Bridge, "winding up the slope through thick woods to the west of the pond and terminating before it leaves the wooded plateau or reaches the rugged sides of Jordan Mountain, at a point commanding a fine view of the ocean. . . ," which was approved by all.[10] As he himself said, "It has been a pleasure to do the various things which I have done in the interest of the community, largely because I felt that they have met with universal approval and endorsement. To continue with any such improvements in the face of even a limited amount of difference of opinion would largely rob the work of its pleasant side."[11] This decision to amend his plans because of minority opposition not only produced an indication of how many people favored the carriage roads but also won him even wider support—which stood him in good stead in later years.

George Dorr must have been deeply concerned at this turn of events. On the one hand, he had a certain personal empathy with the wilderness view. On the other, the controversy threatened the loss of a major supporter and benefactor, which in turn would jeopardize his all-consuming vision for a great park. He need not have worried; far from retreating, Rockefeller was already deeply engrossed in planning another series of carriage roads that Dorr had discussed with him, including several within park jurisdiction. One of these new carriage roads would go from the Bar Harbor side of the park, past Eagle Lake, to Jordan Pond. It would connect the northern and southern sections of the park and would provide access for rangers as well as for carriages and riders. JDR Jr. spent most of the summer of 1921 doing surveys and reconnaissance in the area with Paul Simpson. In July 1922, he sent Dorr the following proposal:

On various occasions for some time past you have told me of your feeling that it was of the utmost importance to connect the driving roads in the national park on this side of the Island with Bar Harbor, so that the people on that side might have easy access hereto. You have intimated that if a road could be built from Jordan Pond, on the west side of the

Pond, through the pass between Jordan and Sargent Mountain and the West Bubble, connection could be made, if necessary, with the old Wood Road which runs from that vicinity out to Eagle Lake Road. . . . Realizing how much it will mean to the horse lovers of Bar Harbor to be able to get into the Park from the Bar Harbor side of the Island, I will contribute whatever amount may be necessary up to $25,000 to enable you to build this connecting link. . . .

Rockefeller then went on to delineate his own ideas as to how the road could be made to continue on through other undeveloped areas and so connect up with some roads that he had already built on his own property:

> If you should decide to go ahead with this work, may I suggest that the road be so laid out, if that should prove to be practicable, as to form the first part of a road around Jordan and Sargent Mountain on the North, joining the present Park roads back of and to the south of Upper Hadlock Pond, should such a road ever be deemed desirable.[12]

This proposal was accepted by Dorr as well as by the government, and the building of this new carriage road established the pattern that characterized JDR Jr.'s work on all roads built on government property. He provided the funds; his engineers, Paul Simpson and later Walters Hill, supervised the work; and his contractors, Clement and Joy, built the road—even though, technically speaking, the work was being done under the aegis of the park and George Dorr was in charge. JDR Jr. himself continued to choose the line of each road and stayed very much abreast of the progress via communications from Dorr and Simpson. He even prepared a contractual letter to Clement for Dorr's signature, spelling out the terms of the work. Over the ensuing years, Rockefeller built many roads in this manner. Since his main interest was in seeing the work go forward, he was always willing to try to find new ways to accomplish this.

If one were to choose a single carriage road in the system to demonstrate technical excellence and superb skill in execution, it would have to be the section of the West Jordan Pond Road that crosses the rock slide (or "tumbledown," as it was called locally) along the west side of Jordan Pond. Anyone looking at the size of the slide, the steepness of the slope, and the massiveness of the boulders would surely have said that it was sheer folly even to contemplate a road at this location. The potential for a major disaster was real. Road work could easily have disturbed the rock slide enough to cause a new movement, resulting in injury or death as well as a public outcry. Remarkably, however, even though both Rockefeller and

A crane rests precariously on the rock slide during the winter of 1923. *C.P. Simpson personal collection*

Looking northward along the finished section of road crossing the "tumbledown."
C.P. Simpson personal collection

Paul Simpson were clearly aware of the project's dangers, they never hesitated. Nor did A.E. Clement, the very able contractor, pale before the challenge. George Dorr, however, was not as confident, and Clement and Simpson bore the brunt of his skepticism as he hovered about the site, making unsolicited suggestions about the grade and alignment of the road. Dorr also wrote about his concerns to JDR Jr.:

> I am anxious to get the utmost possible done this autumn on the rock fall section so that it can be finished in the spring and a road be shown across it next June that will not provoke criticism through being seen in an unfinished state or need to be justified.
>
> I crossed the rock fall on leaving the section Mr. Clement is at work upon and studied it from the construction point of view. No blasting can be done upon it, lest it jar the often delicately balanced rocks and bring them down. In cases where rocks have to be removed to obtain a level road-bed others above that they have helped support will have to be secured by irons or cement, and in places considerable retaining walls will have to be built where the descent is abrupt. It is a critical piece of work both from the engineering and landscape points of view. I plan to spend myself considerable time upon it, consulting as the work goes on with Mr Simpson.
>
> . . . It is the section of the work now planned that is most liable to attack, on the ground that Mr. Walcott took of disturbing a natural scenic feature, and it is from my own point of view as superintendent the section most important to secure for Park connection and control.[13]

In his reply, Rockefeller acknowledged Dorr's concerns: "I note what you say about the problems in crossing the rock slide. You are right in feeling that too great care cannot be exercised in building this particular piece of road. . . . [G]o ahead with the work as rapidly as you wisely can."[14]

Fortunately, the work proceeded without incident or public protest, and in 1926 this road reached the old Wood Road at Eagle Lake. However, there was one casualty; A.E. Clement, the contractor for this section of the road, was relieved of his duties after he finished his section of the work. Over the years, JDR Jr. had gradually added more structure to his system as his land holdings grew bigger and the road work became more extensive, and by 1924, he had a resident superintendent, S.F. Ralston, to oversee his house and private estate. In June of that year, on the recommendation of Charles Heydt, his assistant in New York, he also established a committee to monitor the progress of the work on the carriage roads. Ralston, A.H. Lynam, and Paul Simpson were all members of the committee. For years, Clement had worked directly with Simpson and JDR Jr., enjoying their complete confidence and support, but now he found the supervision of the committee, plus the interference of Dorr, impossible to handle. His insistence on completing the job as he saw fit, in spite of the committee's instructions, brought about his demise.

JDR Jr. did not interfere on behalf of Clement, but he did make a special point of reviewing the West Jordan Pond Road on his spring visit to Maine and writing to Clement to express admiration for Clement's work and his superior skills as a road builder:

> My dear Mr. Clement,
>   I was at Seal Harbor last week, but only for two or three days, and was unable to see you as I had hoped. I went over your road from one end to the other, and was more than ever impressed with its great beauty and grandeur. The view of Jordan Pond and the ocean, as one comes south, away to the north of Deer Brook Bridge, is beautiful beyond description.
>   The work which you have done on the road, particularly at the slide and both sides of it, is such work as it would be difficult to find the equal of any place. The road will long stand as a monument to your road-building ability. Since I did not have an opportunity of doing so in person, I am taking this occasion to express my satisfaction with this road.
>   . . . It is a pleasure to speak thus unqualifiedly of what you have accomplished.[15]

It must have been a bitter pill for Clement to swallow, but at least he could have the satisfaction of knowing that his work was appreciated and that his last, and by far the most difficult, job for JDR Jr. had been a success.

At the same time that JDR Jr. had taken up Dorr's suggestion for a park carriage road on the western side of Jordan Pond, he also proposed that an automobile road be constructed on the eastern side of the pond. This seemed quite startling and out of character, but since he had accepted the inevitability of the automobile on

The first park motor road, built along the east side of Jordan Pond in the 1920s, is the Jordan–Bubble Pond Road (also called Mountain Road locally). *C.P. Simpson personal collection*

Mount Desert and had witnessed the resultant growing popularity of the island, he understood the importance of carefully planning for the use and limitations of cars within park boundaries. He told Dorr that he would be willing to donate up to $150,000 to finance the construction of this first park motor road, which he called the Jordan–Bubble Pond Road. It would start from the Bar Harbor–Somesville town road (now Route 233) and proceed southward, passing between Cadillac Mountain and The Bubbles to join an existing town road at the south end of Jordan Pond next to the Jordan Pond House. Interestingly, he included this offer with the carriage-road plan as part of an entire package that the government could accept or reject all of a piece. Thus he signaled his seriousness about the motor road as well as the carriage roads.

In June 1922, Stephen T. Mather, the park service director, and Arno B. Cammerer, the assistant director, arrived at Mount Desert from Washington to go over the entire plan and visit the sites of the proposed roads. After their stay, Cammerer submitted a lengthy report to Mather in which he made several prophetic comments about the park. These remarks were very much in line with JDR Jr.'s views about the importance of making national parks accessible to larger numbers of people. Cammerer wrote:

> It is to be borne in mind that the great mass of visitors to a national park do not desire walking trips over rugged territory or strenuous climbs; for such, youth and activity, the habit and love of exercise, are necessary. For the older, the less strong and active, or less strenuously inclined, who are the vast majority, means must be provided making reasonably accessible the features of special interest and beauty in the park. Were these, in such a system as Superintendent Dorr has now planned, to be added to the Park's already extensive foot-trail system, I venture to predict that Layafette National Park will become the popular place of resort for lovers of nature and landscape to the eastward of the Great Lakes and Mississippi.

Later in the same report, he spoke of a proposed motor road up Cadillac Mountain that, although not yet in this plan, both JDR Jr. and Dorr had foreseen as inevitable:

> Neither you [Mather] nor I had time to follow the route of the proposed motor road to the top of Cadillac Mountain, or to climb that mountain, but anyone who has climbed any one of the major mountain masses will come to the sure conviction that a road for motorists should lead to the top of at least one of the mountains so that those who cannot climb may get opportunity to receive the inspiration and feel the exaltation of spirit that come with an hour spent on the breeze-swept hills with their superb views over sea and island, losing themselves in far distances. If one good motor road to the top of Cadillac Mountain is not provided in this plan, it will inevitably come though popular insistence in the future.[16]

Coping stones in place
along the first motor road.
*C.P. Simpson personal
collection*

JDR Jr. had already expressed his views on the same subject in
a 1920 letter to George Pepper:

> Since there was once a carriage road to the top of Green [Cadillac]
> Mountain, I should think it not improbable that some day it would be
> rebuilt or a new road built for automobiles. That people who cannot walk
> or conveniently drive should be able to go to the top of one of the
> mountains seems to me not inappropriate or unreasonable. If such a road
> were constructed, I should think it would be the best possible argument
> against the construction of any road, whether for automobile or horses,
> to the top or near the top of any of the other mountains in the Park.[17]

However, this Cadillac Summit road was not included in the
plan—just yet.

The rest of the new plan was approved by the government, and
all went well until construction began on the Jordan–Bubble Pond
motor road in the fall of 1923. When it became public knowledge, a
new storm of protest burst from the summer community, engendered by the very idea of a motor road within park boundaries.

This time, George Pepper launched his attack from Washington
as a United States senator from Pennsylvania. It is not difficult to
imagine his bitterness and sense of betrayal on discovering that
even more roads were being constructed, this time threatening to
bring cars through the very heart of the beloved wilderness so many
had worked to save. His sense of disillusion resulted in part from the
inevitable outcome of the efforts of those dedicated early conservationists. In the act of saving what they loved for future generations,
they were creating something of such value and desirability that it
was already drawing the large numbers of people from whom they

were trying to protect it. The situation was rapidly changing. The acquired lands were no longer essentially a private preserve, as they once had been; they were part of a public park belonging to the federal government. The summer visitors were no longer rugged pioneers slipping unnoticed through the forest, and there was no way they could keep the park exclusively for themselves. Also, the demands and obligations of a public park were far different from those of a private preserve; many more people were involved in the decision-making process and there were many more issues to consider regarding public use and safety. The whole project was growing into something they had not anticipated and therefore were totally unprepared to accept.

Herbert Gleason, a lecturer on national parks and the park inspector under Interior Secretary Lane, captured some of these feelings in an article he wrote for the *Boston Evening Transcript* in August 1924:

> . . . Protests were especially emphatic from the view-point of many of the summer residents, who had long enjoyed the blissful quiet and primitive beauty of the island. They freely stated their fear that the proposed development would bring in a "peanut crowd" of the Coney Island type, and that the park would speedily be littered with egg shells, banana peels, old tin cans. It was even reported that the park was to be "grid-ironed" with roads and its natural beauty irretrievably lost. Some of those who were better informed as to the details of the plan, while not objecting to the road going to the summit of Cadillac Mountain, opposed its being continued through to Jordan Pond, claiming that it would drive away much of the wild life of the region where plants of an unusually rare and interesting character had taken refuge.[18]

JDR Jr., on the other hand, had been thinking and planning all along for this development to occur. On one occasion in another park, when an associate was complaining about a paved road running through a particularly scenic park valley, he said, "What are these parks for, Mr. Chorley? The average American can't afford to go into the secluded areas or to have private trips into the parks. He must travel on such a highway. That's the whole point of the national park system."[19]

Freeman Tilden, a well-known conservation writer and park historian, had this to say about the differences in perception between JDR Jr. and his opponents:

> . . . from the very first of his association with those other conservationists, Mr. Rockefeller had a rather different notion as to what the future of the park and the island might be.
> With the profoundest respect for those who had preceded him, I believe it is true that there was this difference: that Mr. Rockefeller

trusted the public to a greater degree than they. If this be so, it was characteristic of him. Despite the fact that he knows perfectly well that we have always with us the vandal and the visigoth, he yet believes that the vast majority of the people will respond reverently to beauty and cultural opportunity. I think the earliest proponents of Acadia *wanted* to share their good fortune with others; but they loved the island so passionately that they were not sure just how far they ought to go.[20]

So, in their outrage and dismay, and without notifying George Dorr or JDR Jr., Senator George Pepper and Harold Peabody, the chair of the Bar Harbor Village Improvement Association, went to Interior Secretary Hubert Work. They demanded that he halt all construction in the park on the new carriage road as well as the proposed motor road. In addition, they also requested a congressional investigation into the matter. Their vivid descriptions of the desecration of the park's woodlands alarmed Work enough that he issued a stay on the construction. However, they had not reckoned with the power or ingenuity of George Dorr.

Remaining steadfast in his support of the new motor road, Dorr first persuaded Work that if he halted construction in the middle of the winter and effectively put whole crews of men out of work, he would have a media event on his hands. Then he further suggested to the National Park Service that a motor road leading off the Jordan–Bubble Pond Road up to the summit of Cadillac be included in the plan. He knew that the inclusion of this long-discussed idea would ensure the support of many state and park officials. Next, using his considerable political skills and innumerable contacts, he began to marshal a formidable defense and proceeded literally to turn the situation around.

It is important to reiterate that the year-round residents, the park officials, and the state political figures had approved of Rockefeller's roads from the start. The carriage roads represented steady work for the islanders—especially during the lean winter months and later during the Depression years—and they were a significant amenity to attract summer visitors to the park. As a result, many people were more than ready to respond to Dorr's plea for help. Dorr managed to persuade a delegation of Maine's political and civic leaders to appear at the hearing on the matter in Washington in March 1924, and numerous civic organizations submitted resolutions favoring continuation of the road construction. Many prominent summer residents also went, including Lincoln Cromwell and George Stebbins. Others—such as Charles Eliot, Beatrix Farrand (the landscape architect who worked with JDR Jr. on the roads), and Maine governor Percival Baxter—wrote letters endorsing the roads. Two hundred twenty permanent residents of Northeast Harbor, Seal

Harbor, and Somesville sent in petitions of support. Among the permanent residents present at the hearing was contractor Chauncey Joy, and Rockefeller also had a lawyer there to apprise him of what was going on.

In the face of this show of force, Pepper—who had political ambitions in the Republican party and in Maine—backed down. Peabody's offensive misfired when he made the mistake of attacking Brown Mountain Road, which also was under construction at this time. Dorr was only too glad to point out to him that it was being built on Rockefeller's private land and therefore was not within government jurisdiction. However, still sensitive to the opposition, Secretary Work declined to make a definitive decision, choosing to wait until the following summer, when he proposed to go to Acadia and examine the situation. In the meantime, he directed that any work in progress be continued. In fact, therefore, Dorr and JDR Jr. were in command of the field. Work on the roads continued through the spring and into the summer of 1924.

This time, JDR Jr. was not in the least conciliatory to his opponents. Having been attacked publicly without warning or prior discussion, he made no offer to stop construction or to work things out through persuasion. Quite the contrary: He collaborated with Dorr behind the scenes to hasten the progress. On March 18, six days before the hearing, Paul Simpson wrote to report on the speed with which the crews were working:

> I have been quite busy perfecting the location of the Jordan–Sargent Mountain road between the sections where Joy and Clement are working—and also the branch to Bar Harbor. We have several crews chopping out these lines. Mr. Dorr is very anxious to have as much as possible chopped out before the date of the hearing in Washington. Just now I am working on the Chasm Brook section—and I will write you further in regard to my studies there. . . .[21]

Not only did Rockefeller continue work on his own roads, he also wrote a letter to Dorr in Washington the very day of the hearing and offered him up to $25,000 toward the construction of the section of the Sargent Mountain road that would be within park property. The letter contains no reference to the hearing, only allusions to the government approval that already had been granted for these roads. He concluded the letter by saying:

> Since Mr. Joy, who has been building this road for me, was approaching the boundary line when I was at Seal Harbor in the fall and on the reopening of the work in the spring will soon reach it, if in fact he has not already done so, I am sending this letter to you at Washington, in the

event that you should desire to continue the road at this time and should not have in hand funds with which to do so.[22]

Over the summer of 1924, Dorr orchestrated an impressive series of official visitations to the park. A visit by Daniel R. Hull, the chief landscape engineer of the National Park Service, was followed by a second visit from National Park Service director Stephen Mather, who left just as Interior Secretary Work arrived. In addition to reviewing the work in progress, both Mather and Work listened carefully to the objections of those who opposed the scheme. Their visit was followed by one from Maine senator Bert M. Fernald, a former Maine governor, and John A. Peters, a prominent U.S. District Court judge from Ellsworth, both of whom were enthusiastic about the development. After all the reports were in, Secretary Work wrote to George Dorr in July 1924, issuing his approval of all the roads, for both carriages and automobiles, that were in the existing plan for the park. He also said, "I see no objection to a motor road to the top of Cadillac Mtn as outlined. . . ." However, as a final precaution, Work did require that any future roads would have to be approved by his office.[23]

In spite of this additional layer of bureaucratic procedure now required for approval, the forces for development of this unique park moved inexorably on. The growing number of Americans seeking the solace of the out-of-doors, the accessibility of northern New England brought about by the mass production of automobiles, and the startling popularity of the beaches, mountains, and forests of Mount Desert—all conspired to necessitate the kind of planning that George Dorr and JDR Jr. were doing.

After the Washington hearing was over, JDR Jr. continued to work on his roads. If anything, his determination to carry out his grand scheme was reinforced by the resistance to it. Having seen that the majority supported his work, and being clear in his own mind that what he was doing was for the larger public good, he no longer made accommodations to those who opposed him. If the scheme took longer than he originally planned, that was not important; it would be completed in the end.

So, he pressed forward with plans to open up new areas on his own lands and worked with George Dorr within the park and on Reservation property, always seeking the best route to reveal the most beautiful vistas and attributes of the landscape. And he continued to maintain the quality of the work, never abandoning his own attention to detail or the consideration he extended to the men who worked for him.

While road construction continued both on the Sargent Mountain Road on JDR Jr.'s private land and on the West Jordan Pond Road in the park, Dorr was also thinking of other possibilities. The HCTPR still held large tracts of land to the west and north of Eagle Lake that remained undeveloped. Dorr had decided to keep these under Reservation jurisdiction, given the volatile political climate, and he suggested that JDR Jr. could extend his roads in that direction. In this way, the work could continue without having to be approved by the National Park Service. JDR Jr. secured permission from the HCTPR in December 1924 to reconstruct the old Wood Road on the west side of Eagle Lake. Dorr's precaution proved to be wise, because when word of this new road got out the following summer, Harold Peabody wrote indignantly to Secretary Work, protesting that new carriage roads were being built on park land in violation of Work's directive. Since the properties were not in fact within park jurisdiction, nothing came of the complaints, but certain summer residents remained uneasy.

In order for the West Eagle Lake carriage road to reach the northern portion of the Reservation lands, it had to cross a town road at the northern end of Eagle Lake. It was decided that the carriage road should pass under the town road, and JDR Jr. began working on the design for the Eagle Lake Bridge. At the same time he went back to work in the park, and several new carriage roads were under discussion with the National Park Service. One was to start from the southern end of Jordan Pond, proceed around the Triad, and run in a northerly direction to Bubble Pond. There another bridge would cross over the park's controversial first motor road, and the carriage road would continue across the southern end of

Eagle Lake Bridge just after completion in 1928.
C.P. Simpson personal collection

Eagle Lake to join up with the roads on the west. In addition, discussions were underway for a road on the eastern side of the lake, to complete the loop around the water.

As a result of Secretary Work's new requirement, the approval process for additional roads in the park had become considerably more complicated. JDR Jr. personally oversaw the procedure to be sure it was carried out properly, writing detailed instructions to Simpson, with copies to his superintendent, S.F. Ralston, and to A.H. Lynam. In a letter to Paul Simpson, he described how it worked:

> It is my purpose to send one of these blueprints to Mr. Cammerer with a letter advising him that I am prepared to finance the construction of these added two pieces of road and the bridge involved. Mr. Cammerer will in turn ask Mr. Dorr for his recommendation in the matter. He will also, in line with informal assurance given by the Secretary of the Interior, ask Mr. Dorr to send copies of these blueprints to the presidents of the several village improvement societies on Mount Desert Island, so that these societies, or other interested friends through them, may be fully advised of what is under consideration and have ample opportunity to express any views in regard thereto. Mr. Cammerer in writing to Mr. Dorr will indicate some date on which the whole matter will be brought to the Secretary of the Interior for consideration and action and prior to which any expressions of opinion pro or con should be received.[24]

No fewer than a dozen blueprints were prepared for the Eagle Lake–Bubble Pond Road and the Triad–Bubble Pond Road so that all parties would be informed. JDR Jr. was also very careful not to mention in these reports any proposed carriage roads that were on either his own or Reservation property, since they did not require the same approval process, and he sought to avoid stirring up unnecessary trouble.

The trouble already was brewing, however. Even though the carriage roads north of Eagle Lake were not included in the blueprints sent to the Bar Harbor Village Improvement Association, knowledge of their possibility had not escaped the group's nervous and watchful eyes. These new plans brought the roads perilously close to their own haunts around Witch Hole and Paradise Hill, and also invaded the wild sanctity of the Bubble Pond valley. This situation sparked the last organized attempt to monitor and control JDR Jr.'s program.

Following the custom of these societies, the members of the association, under their new president, Episcopal bishop William Lawrence, formed a committee to address the issue. Taking the offensive by making a proposal of their own, they decided to do a study of the whole island from the recreational point of view, hoping by this to rally support for their position and regain control of the course of development of the park and wilderness areas. Introducing the report, Lawrence wrote an impassioned statement:

> Will the Island of Mt Desert become more beautiful and attractive or less so as the years pass? The answer depends upon us who, whether for twelve months or two, live upon the Island; and . . . love it and would do much to conserve its beauties. . . . This report with its maps and suggestions is a challenge to every person upon the Island to take part in a United Movement for its conservation.[25]

Charles Eliot II, the grandson of Harvard's president, was engaged to do the study in the fall of 1926. A young landscape architect with the National Capital Park and Planning Commission in Washington, Eliot had spent time on Mount Desert with his family. Besides noting his professional qualifications, the committee must have hoped that Eliot's Washington connections would prove useful in pleading their cause. However, this did not prove to be the case.

Before the study was even begun, the group ran into trouble. Bishop Lawrence requested a meeting with JDR Jr. in the fall of 1926 to acquaint him with what they were doing and to see whether they could enlist his support. Rockefeller understood immediately that what they wanted was to preempt the leadership of park development and disrupt his road-building program—under the guise of soliciting his cooperation. He reacted accordingly, and described what happened in a letter to Arno Cammerer:

> . . . I have said frankly to Bishop Lawrence and Mr. Eliot that after hearing from them what their plan is, I cannot agree as to its feasibility or wisdom. To undertake to get out of the diverse ownership interests of this Island an agreement on a common plan for the development of the Island seems to me utterly impossible. . . .
> I have, therefore, told these gentlemen that since my judgement did not approve of their program, I obviously could not cooperate with them in it. I am confirmed in my feeling that this committee was organized for the sole purpose of preventing or at least delaying as long as possible the further construction of any roads. . . .[26]

In his reply, Cammerer made it clear that not only was he in agreement with Rockefeller, he did not think much of Eliot's ideas:

> The information you impart concerning the visits of Bishop Lawrence and Mr. Eliot is interesting, and I feel that without a doubt your observations are correct. I have had to listen to several "fool" suggestions made by Mr. Eliot. . . . However, I told him I had no control over his committee, nor over what they desired to do, and whatever they did was on their own responsibility. . . .[27]

In spite of this setback and the fact that they had the support of neither JDR Jr. nor the National Park Service, the Bar Harbor Village Improvement Association pressed on with their report. The completed study, entitled *The Future of Mount Desert Island,* was published and distributed privately in 1928.

In the study, Eliot argued that the future health of the whole island was bound up in the future of the park, and therefore it was in everyone's interest to have a generally agreed-upon plan. He also attempted to make an alliance with the park by quoting from the official park policy issued by Secretary Work in 1925, to the effect that "all improvements [in national parks] should be carried out in accordance with a preconceived plan developed with special reference to the preservation of the landscape," and proposing that his study could constitute such a plan because, he alleged, none had yet been formulated by the officials in charge of the park.

Eliot's plan called for more than doubling the park's 1927 boundaries and for establishing ten wilderness zones within the expanded area, based primarily on their "typical" scenic value, their "beauty, solitude, remoteness, even romanticism," as well as their ecological importance. He argued that these areas, which included the major mountaintops and some of the marshy areas northwest of Eagle Lake, should be accessible only to those "people who are 'wood-wise' and who can appreciate without destroying." He continued: "The introduction of large-scale man-made objects such as buildings, roads, etc., should be avoided as far as possible. There can be no doubt but that walking is the best way to see and appreciate this kind of area and, therefore, footpaths and trails are the most suitable means of access."[28]

This line of reasoning led inevitably to the conclusion that there should be no more carriage roads, and in fact a whole section of the study clearly outlined the arguments for and against the roads that had been voiced over the previous years (see Appendix D). It concluded by arguing that the cessation of further construction was warranted because of the slight use of the existing carriage roads, the few remaining truly wild areas, the scars resulting from carriage-road construction, the potential threat of automobile use, and stated park policy against overdevelopment of roads.

JDR Jr. could not have taken kindly to this latest salvo from his opponents. From his point of view, the report contained numerous contradictions and thinly veiled attacks. First of all, even though it was true that there had never been an official park plan for Acadia, JDR Jr. had very explicit plans for the park that he had been working on for years in collaboration with George Dorr—plans that had the very clear approval of the National Park Service. So, in fact, it was not the lack of a plan that was considered objectionable but rather the extent of JDR Jr.'s scheme. With regard to Eliot's proposed expansion of the park boundaries, by far the majority of the areas he indicated were already owned by JDR Jr., had carriage roads on them, and were open to the public. There was a certain presumption here in Eliot's reference to them without any indication of their ownership and present use. In regard to the carriage roads themselves, Eliot talked simultaneously about how little used they were and yet how they would be the cause of bringing in too many of the wrong type of people, who would not appreciate the wilderness. Finally, he proposed that the wilder mountaintop areas be left accessible only to those who could use foot trails, while at the same time suggesting recreational "centers" attracting larger numbers of people than either Rockefeller or Dorr had ever contemplated. One of these centers was to be at Jordan Pond, where he mentioned installing tennis courts, a swimming pool, and a golf course. With all this, it is hardly surprising that Cammerer took issue with Eliot and his report.

Although it is not clear how Eliot's report was distributed and what the reactions were, its impact certainly was limited. It was obvious that Secretary Work's directive for review of road-building projects did not include the power to halt the roads entirely. Eventually, the Eliot study apparently just faded away. But during this period, there was some discussion of the matter in the *Bar Harbor Times,* after which JDR Jr. received more letters, primarily in support of what he had done. One gentleman, Samuel Drury, the headmaster of St. Paul's School in Concord, New Hampshire, wrote JDR Jr. a note at the end of every summer for more than ten years expressing his family's appreciation for the carriage roads. Visiting and local professional associations also wrote in support, including the Maine State Highway Commission, the American Legion Post in Bar Harbor, and the Bar Harbor Board of Trade (later the Chamber of Commerce).

All during this period of controversy, the road work continued, and by 1928 the road system was moving northward under the completed Eagle Lake Bridge up toward Duck Brook, Witch Hole Pond, and Paradise Hill, which became, in JDR Jr.'s words, "the grand terminus" of the system. These roads included panoramic vistas from the top of Paradise Hill out over Frenchman Bay as well as more intimate views where the road skirted the edges of three small ponds. Duck Brook Bridge, the eleventh one built in the system, was under construction at the same time, and the Bubble Pond Bridge, completed in 1928, connected the two segments of the Bubble Pond carriage road. By 1929, road work was begun on the eastern side of Eagle Lake to complete the loop around the water.

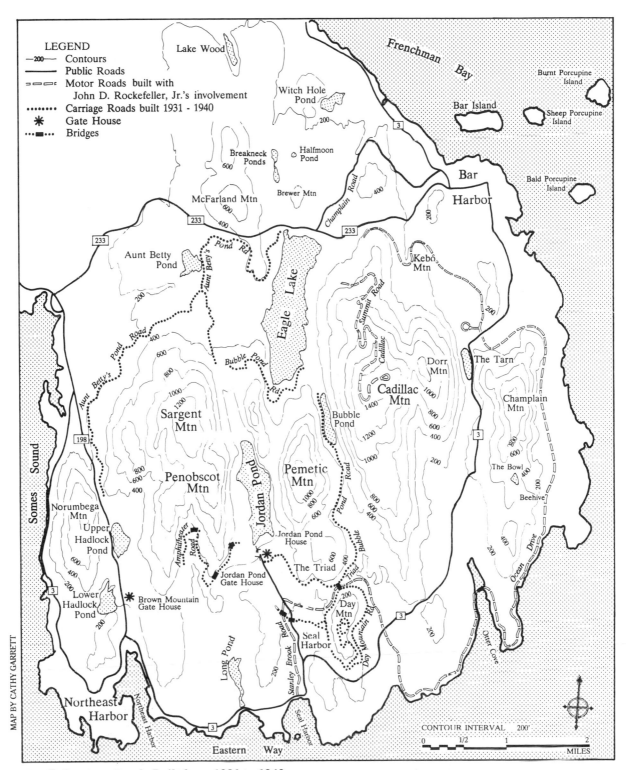

LEGEND
- ―200― Contours
- ——— Public Roads
- ─ ─ ─ Motor Roads built with John D. Rockefeller, Jr.'s involvement
- ••••••• Carriage Roads built 1931 - 1940
- ✱ Gate House
- •••■••• Bridges

Lake Wood

Frenchman Bay

Witch Hole Pond

Burnt Porcupine Island

Bar Island

Sheep Porcupine Island

Breakneck Ponds

Halfmoon Pond

600

Brewer Mtn

McFarland Mtn

Bar Harbor

Bald Porcupine Island

Champlain Road

233

400

200

233

233

Kebo Mtn

Aunt Betty Pond

Aunt Betty's Pond Rd

Eagle Lake

Summit Road

Cadillac

Dorr Mtn

The Tarn

200

Aunt Betty's Pond Road

400

200

600

Bubble Pond Rd

1000

1200

Cadillac Mtn

1400

1000

800

600

400

Champlain Mtn

800

600

3

198

Sargent Mtn

800

600

400

Bubble Pond

1200

1000

200

The Bowl

400

200

Penobscot Mtn

Jordan Pond

Pemetic Mtn

1000

800

600

Pond Road

800

400

Beehive

400

Somes Sound

Norumbega Mtn

Upper Hadlock Pond

600

400

Amphitheater Road

Jordan Pond House

Jordan Pond Gate House

The Triad

Bubble

Triad

200

Ocean Drive

3

Lower Hadlock Pond

200

✱ Brown Mountain Gate House

Day Mtn

Seal Harbor

Day Mountain Rd

3

200

Otter Cove

3

Stanley Brook Road

Long Pond

200

Seal Harbor

Northeast Harbor

Northeast Harbor

3

Eastern   Way

MAP BY CATHY GARRETT

CONTOUR INTERVAL   200'

0   1/2   2

MILES

Map 7: Carriage Roads Built from 1931 to 1940

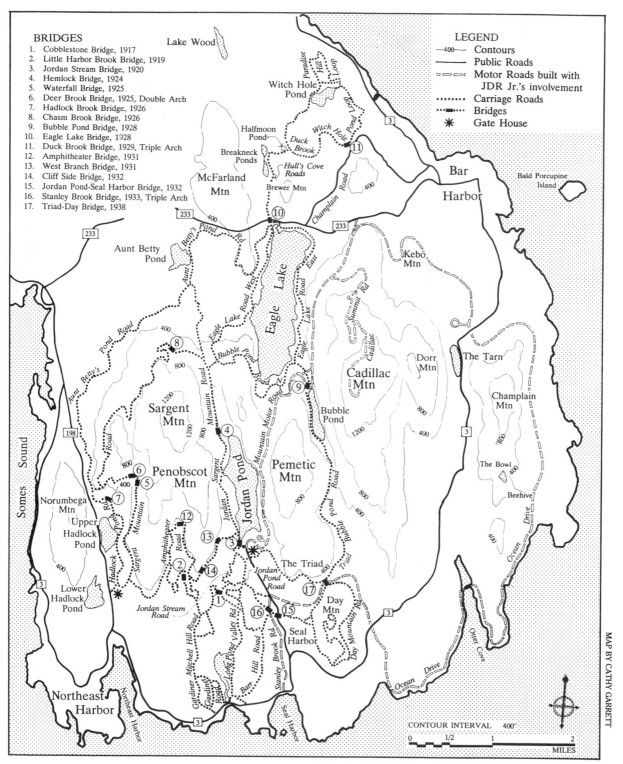

BRIDGES
1. Cobblestone Bridge, 1917
2. Little Harbor Brook Bridge, 1919
3. Jordan Stream Bridge, 1920
4. Hemlock Bridge, 1924
5. Waterfall Bridge, 1925
6. Deer Brook Bridge, 1925, Double Arch
7. Hadlock Brook Bridge, 1926
8. Chasm Brook Bridge, 1926
9. Bubble Pond Bridge, 1928
10. Eagle Lake Bridge, 1928
11. Duck Brook Bridge, 1929, Triple Arch
12. Amphitheater Bridge, 1931
13. West Branch Bridge, 1931
14. Cliff Side Bridge, 1932
15. Jordan Pond-Seal Harbor Bridge, 1932
16. Stanley Brook Bridge, 1933, Triple Arch
17. Triad-Day Bridge, 1938

Lake Wood

LEGEND
—400— Contours
——— Public Roads
– – – Motor Roads built with
       JDR Jr.'s involvement
········· Carriage Roads
·■·■·■· Bridges
✳ Gate House

MAP BY CATHY GARRETT

CONTOUR INTERVAL   400'

0   1/2   1   2
                                          MILES

Map 8: Bridges of the Carriage-Road System

The rustic Bubble Pond Bridge was built in 1928 to carry the West Eagle Lake carriage road over the park motor road. *C.P. Simpson personal collection*

All in all, seven bridges were built between 1922 and 1929, and many miles of road were constructed, creating an enormously expanded road system that opened up many beautiful areas of the park. It was now possible to go by carriage or horse from Northeast Harbor, past Seal Harbor, on to Bar Harbor, and back—all without having to follow the same route. In the process, one could go along several beautiful lakes, circle Sargent and Jordan mountains, drive over a rock slide, and enjoy spectacular views of the ocean, the mountains, and surrounding woodlands.

Following this period of intense activity, the emphasis shifted during the final years of road building from 1930 to 1940, although the pace of road building did not decline. Rather than extending the carriage-road system into new areas, JDR Jr. was mainly making connections between existing roads, finishing work he had started, designing and building the two gate houses, and spending a great deal of time on roadside cleanup and planting.

In 1930, he recommended work on the Amphitheater Road, abandoned ten years earlier in deference to the objections of George Pepper and other summer residents. This segment starts at the southern end of Jordan Pond and climbs steadily along the flank of Penobscot Mountain toward the deep bowl-shaped ravine known as The Amphitheater. Two bridges are placed along the way. West Branch Bridge has a tall, narrow arch and curves to fit the mountainside. Cliffside Bridge is massive, its modified barrel arch springing right out of the rock and its fortresslike abutments stretching 230 feet along the cliff. Halfway up the mountain, the road turns north to reveal startlingly expansive views into the Amphitheater ravine. Continuing around the inner edge of the ravine, close against the mountain, the road holds the traveler as if in a theater and affords broad views over the forest-filled basin toward the sea. A third bridge—Amphitheater Bridge, at the apex of the ravine—crosses a tumbling mountain stream with a lovely waterfall. It is not hard to understand why Rockefeller felt that this road was essential to the whole system.

JDR Jr. also began planning a long stretch of road north and west of Sargent Mountain to link the northern end of Eagle Lake with an existing road along the edge of Upper Hadlock Pond. This route would explore stands of hemlock, meadow, and marshland, and skirt the edge of a little body of water called Aunt Betty Pond, from which the road took its name. The whole stretch had a very different character from the scenic roads above it. However, in order for the road to ascend the flank of Sargent Mountain and connect with the Sargent–Jordan road, it would be necessary to traverse a rather steep slope. After the preliminary reconnaissance, Paul Simpson offered three alternatives, which were spelled out in five letters he and JDR Jr. exchanged over a four-week period. These letters are very revealing of JDR Jr.'s precision and his commitment to finding the proper solution.

"I much prefer route three," he wrote, "for its location, its beauty, its point of arrival and its directness, two being the compromise that gives us the beauty of the valley but takes us so far North and out of the way. . . . If we turn to Route One, it would be because it is the shortest and the best grade, although the most uninteresting." He was, however, concerned about whether the grade would be too difficult: "I fear the grade of Three is prohibitive, 7% for 1500 is bad. Have we any piece of horse road that is comparable to that?"[29] In the end, even though they both recalled other successful portions of road with comparable conditions, it was agreed that they would postpone making a choice until JDR Jr. could study the situation during his summer visit. As always, he based his final decision on direct observation of the site in order not to compromise the work. On-site reconnaissance confirmed the feasibility of the choice Rockefeller favored, and the road was built along that route.

During the 1930s, JDR Jr. was contemplating building three other sections of road as well as preparing the designs for the two gate houses that would mark the entrances to the carriage-road system. One section, the Day Mountain Road, was to go from Barr Hill on JDR Jr.'s property across Stanley Brook to the top of Day Mountain. This carriage road circles a small hill behind Seal Harbor and offers views of the harbor to the south and the larger mountains behind. It was built in sections over a ten-year period. The first portion, constructed during the early 1930s, went from Barr Hill

The triple-arched Stanley
Brook Bridge in 1933, soon
after it was completed.
*C.P. Simpson personal
collection*

across Stanley Brook and under the Seal Harbor–Jordan Pond town
road. The Stanley Brook Bridge, which carries the carriage road over
the brook, has three Roman arches: one for the motor road, one for
the brook, and a third for the Seaside Trail leading from Seal Harbor
to the Jordan Pond House. The Jordan Pond Road bridge is so
inconspicuous as an underpass that it is hard to detect from the
motor road.

By 1935, the surveys and alignment had been completed for yet
another segment encircling Day Mountain. The final summit road up
the little mountain was completed in 1940. This last piece is the only
road in the entire system that runs to the top of a mountain, in
contradiction to JDR Jr.'s stated intentions. However, Day Mountain
is low, 583 feet at its peak, and is so situated that it does not intrude
on the views from any other peaks.

The other two proposed carriage-road sections, known as the
Kebo Valley roads, were to have allowed rides from the northeast
corner of Eagle Lake, proceeding east past Newport Mountain and
the Kebo Valley and through the Great Meadow to the Sieur de Monts
Spring. George Dorr was very much in favor of these roads, as the
Great Meadow was a favorite of his. He originally acquired it in hopes
of developing a wildflower garden there, but the idea never came to
fruition, and JDR Jr. eventually bought the property from him.
Neither Kebo Valley road was built, although all the surveys and
alignments were made and the roads were staked out by engineers
Hill and Simpson.

JDR Jr. also became involved in the planning of the park's
motor roads during the 1930s. He worked with the park in designing

The Jordan Pond Road
Bridge under construction,
and after completion in
1932. *C.P. Simpson
personal collection*

and building the scenic road up Cadillac Mountain, the Ocean Drive route, and the Stanley Brook Road to Jordan Pond. These roads—designed and built according to the same principles as the carriage roads—are the centerpieces of the Acadia National Park motor-road system. Without JDR Jr.'s unwavering attention and persistence, it is doubtful whether Ocean Drive would have come to pass at all, as once again there was substantial opposition to the plan from a few summer residents which delayed the completion of the road for several years. The *Bar Harbor Times* chronicled the controversy, and in a letter to the paper one opponent wrote, "The danger to our Island lies not so much in one particular new road, but from a policy of general road building whereby section after section of our woods and mountains become invaded by clouds of dust, honks of horns, remains of picnics from flivver tourists and smells of gasoline."[30]

JDR Jr. calmly withstood the controversy and remained steadfast in his views of how Ocean Drive should be built. As he said to Cammerer, "I am simply not interested except on the terms of my original offer. . . . People are interested in blocking something which they think I have my heart set on doing. If they know I am indifferent, then the proposal begins to be considered on its merits; and when, as in this case, the merits are found to be very considerable, like all other blessings they brighten as they take their flight."[31] The road was finally built as he envisioned it.

JDR Jr. also worked on the alignment of the road up Cadillac Mountain and made sure that the treatment of the banks and edges was up to the standards of his other roads.

As work on the carriage-road system drew to completion, Rockefeller began turning his vast land holdings, with their miles of carriage roads, over to the park. By this time, he had worked on the development of Acadia and the carriage-road system for nearly thirty years and had realized most of his vision for a unique national park. He had acquired land to fill out the park boundaries from Frenchman Bay to the Atlantic Ocean and from Brown Mountain to Ocean Drive. He had built fifty-seven miles of carriage roads and many bridges to open up the inner regions to visitors.

He began this transfer gradually, starting in the early 1930s, by first giving the park his lands around Otter Creek, the Brown Mountain Lodge, and all the acreage around it, including Upper Hadlock Pond and Little Brown Mountain. Then in 1935, in his sixty-first year, he decided to relinquish control of his beloved project completely. He wrote to Interior Secretary Harold Ickes indicating that he was ready to divest himself of the major portion of his remaining lands (see Appendix F). This procedure took until the early 1940s and included all the remaining land containing carriage roads: Day Mountain, the Paradise Hill area, the Kebo Valley acreage, the Jordan Pond Lodge, and Jordan Pond House (which he also owned). He indicated to the park that the construction of the Kebo Valley roads was up to them, and although his agreement with the park made provision for him to build future carriage roads in the park, none were ever constructed.

As part of the agreement he specifically asked the park service to guarantee that the carriage roads would be closed to automobile traffic for at least twenty-five years from the time of transfer. He clearly stated this request and his reasons for specifying a limited time period in a letter to Interior Secretary Lyman Wilbur in 1932:

> If my offer of this land is accepted, I feel it should be with the understanding clearly set forth in the deed that for a period of at least twenty-five years from the date of the gift the horse roads now on this land or which may hereafter be built thereon will be open only for the use of horses, horse-drawn vehicles and pedestrians and not for motor traffic, except with my consent or that of my heirs or assigns given on the recommendation and at the request of the National Park Service, and except also when necessary for general road and roadside maintenance, repair and construction purposes, fire fighting and in case of accident. While it would be my hope that these roads would continue for the long future to justify themselves as horse roads only, I would not be willing nor would it be in the public interest were it possible, to seek to impose my views in the matter for all time.[32]

Today, the carriage roads remain closed to automobiles, as Rockefeller desired.

Years later, he summed up the philosophy of work that had carried him through this project to his biographer, Raymond Fosdick:

> When I thought a thing was worth doing, I made up my mind that the annoyances, the obstacles, the embarrassments had to be borne because the ultimate goal was worthwhile. If I started a course, I expected to go on with it, and the obstacles in the way of criticism, misrepresentation, etc., became merely details. . . . I thought the projects through pretty carefully, as you know, but once embarked on a course I expected to see it through at whatever cost.[33]

CHAPTER 5

Practical Matters

Constructing the Carriage Roads

The engineering of the Mount Desert carriage roads is a story in itself. The alignment of the roads, vertical and horizontal, was done geometrically, and was carefully planned to allow smooth driving and easy riding. The radius of every curve was carefully worked out so they would be comfortable for carriages. Each gradient was engineered so that no place would be too steep for easy access. Because JDR Jr. understood the principles of engineering, he was able to orchestrate all of this. He could realize his aesthetic and environmental ideals on the ground. So that rare event in modern-day road construction occurred: the marriage of aesthetics and engineering, science and art, resulting in beautiful and harmonious roadways that lie lightly upon the land.

JDR Jr.'s correspondence with his engineers, Charles and Paul Simpson, with his superintendent, S.F. Ralston, and with each of the contractors reveals the extent of his technical knowledge about road building. He was equally at home talking about grading or the radius of the curves or the stations, as this interchange over the roads north of Long Pond illustrates: "I walked over the road which you are building the other day," he wrote to contractor Clement, "and reached the conclusion that the 16 ft. traveled width should stop at about Station 12, from which to Station 24 the road will be a bridle path like the one along the Jordan Stream."[1] And to Paul Simpson he wrote, "I understand from your letter that you have all the data necessary with you and that it is only a question of your being able to take the time to plat the rest of the road line and establish a grade line on the profile."[2]

JDR Jr. insisted that the carriage roads be built to the standards of the best rural roads of that time—"broken-stone roads," as they were called. (They were known locally as "rock-filled roads.") Although much more expensive than the earth roads commonly constructed, they were extremely durable.[3] Specifications for the roads were developed by JDR Jr. in consultation with Charles and Paul Simpson. Over the years, the basic requirements remained the same, although they were adapted to the particular situation of each road segment. In 1918, JDR Jr. wrote to Clement, enclosing a copy of

Opposite: **An early mechanized crane moving rocks.** *C.P. Simpson personal collection*

111

his specifications for a new section of road from the Gardiner–Mitchell Hill Road westward toward the Upper Hadlock Pond Road. His meticulous specs described the construction process:

> The road to be built shall be what is known locally as a rock filled road, with a top surface of clay and bank gravel, such as may be found in the vicinity of the work. . . . The road shall be built true to line and grade as established on the ground by the engineer or as shown on plans, with no humps, hollows, yanks or crocks, and the lines, particularly on curves, shall be true and even. All wet and low places shall be filled with rock. . . . The foundation shall be of broken rock finished with at least 4 inches of small rock and to be crowned 8 inches from edge to center of road. Upon this will be put a light coating of fine screenings or coarse gravel sufficient to fill up the spaces between the stones so that the top dressing will not sift through.

The specifications went on to describe the standard width of the road and how the crown was to be made:

> The road shall be 16 feet in traveled width inside the gutters, fences or walls. . . . and will be crowned so as to be 8 inches higher in the centre than at the edges. This crowning to be even and to be made in the rock fill and verified before the top surface is put on.[4]

This sixteen-foot road width was the standard for the great majority of the carriage roads, although a few of the roads were only ten feet wide, principally those connecting with the bridle paths built by the Northeast Harbor Village Improvement Society in the Upper Hadlock Pond area. JDR Jr. considered these narrower roads bridle paths, as they were not wide enough for two carriages to pass easily.

His youngest son, David Rockefeller, recalls going with his father to watch the road work in progress. He remembers his father's meticulous attention to what was going on and how he checked on the size of the rocks used to form the base of the road bed, insisting that the pieces be uniform. David also talks about his own fascination with the hand-powered equipment used during the early construction years. There were derricks with grappling hooks to move boulders around the site and slides pulled by horses to move the stone. Most of the stone was cut by hand right on the site, and David watched as the men hand-drilled holes into the bedrock and inserted dynamite to blast away the rock where the road had to be cut into the mountainside. Later, JDR Jr. added mechanical equipment, but always with an eye to the cost. Steamrollers to replace horse-drawn rollers in finishing the road surface, small tractors, and mechanized derricks were introduced in the twenties. The first steam shovel was

Hand derricks and horse-drawn stone sleds were used in early carriage-road construction. *C.P. Simpson personal collection*

purchased to expedite the difficult and dangerous work across the Jordan Pond rock slide.[5]

Cutting the road line through the woods before laying the roadbed was the most sensitive part of the process. Great care was taken to ensure that the line went just the right way and that the surrounding environment was disturbed as little as possible. "Be sure your men cut trees for too narrow a roadway rather than too wide a one, as they cut down into the valley," JDR Jr. wrote to Clement. "I want to spare every tree possible, without spoiling the line of the road, just as I did along the Jordan Stream bridle path."[6]

The drainage systems on the roads are masterpieces of design and craftsmanship. JDR Jr. believed that drainage was fundamental to good road construction, so he engineered an extensive drainage system into the roads. "My experience in road building," he wrote to George Dorr, "has been that the greatest economy in maintenance is obtained by the greatest care and thoroughness in designing and constructing the drainage system. This I am sure you have also found to be true."[7]

The eight-inch crown on the roads ensured that water would drain off into the ditches and culverts on either side and be dispersed back into the ground. The two-foot-wide drainage ditches—in some places lined with stone or cut right into granite ledge—run along one or both sides of the roads to carry the runoff to the culverts. In one instance, near Hemlock Bridge, a rushing seasonal stream comes down a steep incline at right angles to the road. The stonework is extended up the stream bed as a series of giant steps that disappear into the woods above and channel the water to the culvert passing under the road.

The culverts, placed every hundred yards, were built directly into the roadbed. Wherever the bed had enough depth, they were built with hand-cut stone on the sides and bottom. Stone lintels were laid over the top, which then was covered with the same kind of gravel used for the rest of the road surface. Otherwise, iron pipes were laid to carry off the water from the ditches under the road. The stone culverts are like miniature bridges under the roads, some even being large enough to crawl through. They were done with the same care as everything else—as though they would be in full view. The whole system makes a fascinating study all in itself, both aesthetically and functionally.

In many places along the carriage roads there are also retaining walls, which were built wherever the roads cut into the side of the mountain or passed by an area with loose rock. Whether constructed of the stone that was blasted out to make way for the road or from quarried stone, they were built with the same precision and care used for the rest of the road. Where these walls are on the upper side of the road, they are engineered to hold back loose earth or rock. Those on the lower side, holding up the roadbed, sometimes are massive, and, when viewed from below, give a dramatic glimpse of just how much intervention was required for building the roads. Now, however, nature has done her work, and the rocks are patterned with multicolored lichens. Shrubbery or trees veil even the most monumental walls.

To protect carriages or riders from going off the side in places where there was a steep drop-off or a high retaining wall, coping stones were set along the edges of the roads. These long lines of stone teeth were placed last, after the drainage system had been

Moving coping stones along the West Jordan Pond Road. *C.P. Simpson personal collection*

installed and the road surface laid. Rockefeller was very precise as to how they should be installed:

> Such stone coping as may be required along the road for safety is to be constructed. . . . I suggest that where this coping is used the stones be set a little distance from each other, say six to twelve inches, in such places as this can be done with safety to traffic. Where closer setting will give a greater feeling of safety, it should be done, although I prefer the wider spacing, so far as appearance is concerned, and at the same time it is less expensive. However it is not my desire to sacrifice safety in any instance.[8]

The specifications for the West Jordan Pond Road further address the character of the coping stones:

> The stones are not to touch but to be separated by about a foot or more or less according to the shape of the stones and how high the wall may be which the coping protects, and are not to be lined up, but put in at irregular angles so as to give a rustic appearance on the roadside.[9]

These stones were also used along the roads at Pocantico Hills and the roads built by JDR Sr. at Forest Hill. But they are less in evidence, because the terrain there is gentler, with rolling hills rather than mountains. The idea, however, was available to be used. On Mount Desert Island they became known familiarly as "Rockefeller's teeth," perhaps because they are so prevalent and line the mountainsides like rows of giant molars.

In order that the roads, when completed, would blend back into the landscape, JDR Jr. insisted that great care be taken to clean away debris and restore the edges and banks:

...All stumps shall be pulled or grubbed out. Brushwood, stumps, tree limbs, etc., must not be cast upon the adjacent land, but shall be formed into piles and burned; stumps and other materials that will not burn must be removed from the work and disposed of to the satisfaction of the owner. All brush or trees accidentally or otherwise thrown upon the adjacent lands must be taken off and disposed of as above described....

Particular care must be taken in the burning of all brush and stumps so as not to scorch or injure growing trees. Any tree so scorched or injured must be taken down at the contractor's expense and disposed of.[10]

Just as he was adamant about seeing that the land and vegetation were injured as little as possible, he was quick to express satisfaction when these requests were carried out. He wrote to Chauncey Joy:

...I am particularly delighted with the careful and thorough way, slow and tedious though it has been, in which you have cleaned up the ledges over which blasted rock had been thrown. This has immensely reduced the visibility of the road scar. The top soil which you are now putting over the rock fills along this stretch of road will in another year or so still further largely obliterate the scar of the road.[11]

In this meticulous and painstaking manner, the roads of Acadia National Park were built, one by one winding their way through the valleys and mountainsides, each attended to by JDR Jr. as if it were the first and only one to be built.

Many people have commented how genuinely at home JDR Jr. was in the work environment. According to Robert Pyle, the director of the Northeast Harbor Library, Rockefeller's ease, his professional knowledge, and his fair treatment of the men gained him a level of acceptance among the year-round residents that was very unusual for summer folk. Some of the old-timers who worked on the road told Pyle that when JDR Jr. was dressed "fancy" and was riding in one of his carriages they knew to address him with formality as "Mr. Rockefeller," but when he showed up in his tweeds and work boots he was "Mr. Junior" and could be approached directly.[12] From JDR Jr.'s point of view, the road crews were largely composed of men with no pretenses who were not out to exploit his wealth or gain favor for their own ends; rather, he and they were engaged in a common pursuit that was the object of their professional pride. Because of this he let down his habitual guard in ways he did not often do in public.

As engineer Victor Layton said in his 1982 *Down East* magazine article on the carriage roads:

Mr. Rockefeller had an intense interest in the progress of the work and came to the sites frequently, attired in baggy pants, a tweed jacket, and a brown felt hat.... He knew most of the men by name and made it a point to remember them. He was open to suggestions from the simplest worker and made many adjustments on the spot, following his special vision of how the project would look in the end.... During the noon break, he often went to the superintendent's tar-paper shack where the plans were kept, so he could examine them and discuss details with the man in charge. "I wish I could take the view with me to New York," he said during a visit at the Amphitheatre Bridge, "it would be nice to see from my office."[13]

Bridge Building—As If Nature Had Put It There

JDR Jr. planned the bridges on the carriage roads to be delightful to the eye, to fit easily and unobtrusively into the terrain, to bring another experience of the landscape to passersby, and to be of the highest quality. In all of these respects he succeeded.

Of the sixteen bridges that JDR Jr. built on the carriage roads, only three have any proximity to the park motor roads, and these carry the horse roads over (or, in one case, under) the motor roads. The other bridges are deep in the woods, settled into the landscape and far from the noise and speed of the automobile. Their solid granite structures fit comfortably into the mountainsides.

Each bridge has its own distinctive character and views. Cobblestone Bridge, the first to be built in 1917, was entirely faced with "natural moss-faced rocks," at the suggestion of Charles Simpson. JDR Jr. heartily agreed, feeling that the bridge would look "less artificial and more harmonious with the surroundings." However, the difficulty of procuring enough rough boulders argued against building any of the other bridges in the same style. Hadlock Brook

Cobblestone Bridge, photographed by Paul Simpson in the 1930s. *C.P. Simpson personal collection*

Duck Brook Bridge under construction in the late 1920s. *C.P. Simpson personal collection*

Bridge, crossing a quiet stream, has a low arch and simple rustic mien. Amphitheater Bridge is the longest, at 235 feet, and rises gracefully to a low peak in the center of its curving wall. Openings in the stone give it a lighter feeling to offset its size and the fifty-foot semi-Gothic arch below. Duck Brook Bridge has steps down to the rushing stream beneath and is the most sophisticated, with its cream-colored stone and corbeled viewing platforms.

Two New York architects worked closely with JDR Jr. to design these structures, and several Maine contractors did the construction with local workers and stonemasons. Welles Bosworth was responsible for most of the earlier bridges, designing ten of them between 1917 and 1928 (see Appendix A). A prominent architect, Bosworth was known, among other things, for his design of the original Classic Revival buildings at the Massachusetts Institute of Technology. He worked with JDR Jr. over a long period, first designing the elaborate Italianate gardens JDR Jr. built for his father at Pocantico Hills between 1908 and 1910. Then, in 1914, he designed the interior of JDR Jr.'s New York City house. Later, after World War I, Bosworth went to Paris to direct the fine restoration work done on Versailles, Fontainebleau, and Rheims Cathedral—all made possible by gifts from JDR Jr. Charles Stoughton did the remaining bridges, working from 1929 to 1933, when the last one was completed over the Stanley Brook motor road. His work on bridge designs for New York's Bronx River Parkway recommended him to Rockefeller in the early 1920s, and he first designed bridges for JDR Jr.'s horse roads in Tarrytown.

JDR Jr.'s bridges do, as he'd hoped, "delight the eye." Their soft pink and gray tones and their rustic character are very much a part of the surrounding granite ledges and woodland scenes. Their design was indirectly influenced by JDR Jr.'s travels in Europe as a young man and by the prevailing interest in rustic design in general. Several were inspired by two particular bridges in Central Park, where Rockefeller went for frequent walks and carriage rides: "Recently I found a rough stone bridge in Central Park," JDR Jr. wrote to Charles Simpson when they were contemplating designs for Little Harbor Brook Bridge in 1919, "which I think a much more beautiful design and which I have had adapted to the requirements of the Little Harbor Brook Crossing."[14] This bridge is at the south end of the park and spans one end of Swan Lake. The same design, which Bosworth used in a modified form and adapted to each particular situation, was used for two other bridges on the carriage roads, the Jordan Stream Bridge at the south end of Jordan Pond and the Hadlock Brook Bridge near Upper Hadlock Pond. In addition, West Branch Bridge was inspired by a bridge with a tall narrow arch in the Ramble that Charles Simpson noticed when he visited Rockefeller in New York to study the bridge over Swan Lake.

All the Maine bridges are made of the native granite and all have barrel or modified Gothic arches. The arch stones are set on end with a keystone at the top. Thirteen of the sixteen bridges have single arches. Deer Brook Bridge on West Jordan Pond Road has two tall, narrow arches; the Stanley Brook Bridge and the Duck Brook Bridge have triple arches. The granite on all of them is rough-cut but beautifully executed, giving them the appearance of both high craftsmanship and informality. The bridge parapets are all low, allowing walkers as well as riders to look out at the views while going across or to lean down and watch the streams and waterfalls below.

Charles W. Stoughton designed eight of the carriage-road bridges. 1931 photo. *C.P. Simpson personal collection*

Jordan Stream Bridge, at the south end of Jordan Pond, was one of three modeled after a bridge in Central Park. *C.P. Simpson personal collection*

Deer Brook Bridge, on the Jordan–Sargent Mountain carriage road, crosses a mountain stream. *C.P. Simpson personal collection*

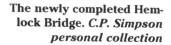

The newly completed Hemlock Bridge. *C.P. Simpson personal collection*

JDR Jr. took great pains to see that each bridge was carefully placed to fit into the landscape. As always, he felt the best way to decide among options was in the field. "It seems to me," he wrote to Paul Simpson, "that it would be desirable for you to stake out the Hemlock bridge in the ground as shown in the drawing, and then write me just how you think it adjusts itself to the natural lay of the land; also what changes in location of stream, side walls or any particular you think would make the bridge better adapted to the place."[15]

He also consulted and listened carefully to the opinions of the men he employed, and he never failed to back them up after the decisions had been made and the work had finally begun: "I note the large cut in the bank necessary in this end of the Waterfall bridge.

Waterfall Bridge is tucked into the landscape on the west side of Parkman Mountain on Sargent Mountain carriage road. *C.P. Simpson personal collection*

Nothing else would suffice, and although you are taking heroic measures, I fully agree with you that you are doing just right."[16] These rugged men were not insensitive to the land themselves, and JDR Jr.'s confidence in their judgment was not misplaced. In the planning stages for the Amphitheater Bridge, Paul Simpson wrote at length to JDR Jr. about plans for saving two large, handsome trees while still siting the bridge to provide the most favorable view up the stream:

> I have been studying further, the bridge site in the Amphitheatre Road at the Little Harbor Brook crossing with a view to make more certain the saving of the two large trees at the site—a 20' hemlock and a 20' pine.... Of course it would be desirable to have the small waterfall above the bridge in line with the axis of the arch—but with this crossing the construction would be rather difficult.[17]

JDR Jr.'s reply:

> It is important to save the trees if we can. It is also important to so locate the bridge that the waterfall will be pleasingly framed by it. The bridge should also be wide enough for comfortable use. Just what compromise may be necessary in order to give the fullest possible consideration to all these points can be determined only on the ground.[18]

The two trees in question are still in evidence today, and the result is a 235-foot-long curving bridge that sweeps across the mountain stream between the two trees, giving a fine view of the waterfall from the top and framing it gracefully from below.

The high quality of construction used for the bridges required a great deal of hand labor carefully executed, but JDR Jr. also made

Great blocks of local granite were quarried for the bridges. *C.P. Simpson personal collection*

full use of contemporary technology. This allowed him wider latitude in design but also the ability to keep the rustic appearance of solid stone construction. The walls and arches rested on huge poured-concrete footings. The internal or load-bearing structure of each bridge is steel-reinforced concrete with steel ties. The arches were first framed in with wooden structures, and finally everything was faced with hand-hewn granite rising up to form the walls, parapets, and turrets. Dirt fill was put in between the walls, and then gravel surface was laid over the top.

In his 1982 article, Victor Layton reflected on the labor expended on these bridges:

> . . . [T]he granite for the bridges was extracted from the ledges near or actually on each construction site. Black powder was used to fracture the rock because it is a slower burning explosive than dynamite. Large slabs were then drilled and cracked with wedges and bars to produce blocks of the right size for the bridges. Afterwards, the blocks were moved by horse- or tractor-drawn stoneboats and lifted onto the cutting platforms—circular, sturdy wood benches with a motorized derrick in the center. The derrick served to turn the blocks as needed for shaping and also to hoist them into their final position on the future bridge. . . .
>
> Dimensions of the finished granite blocks were transposed from the plans to the rough stone with a stonemason's scale, and the lines were drawn with a soft redwood dowel, which drew a finer line than chalk. . . . An elegant arch required the most exacting work and was shaped over a frame of planks and timbers with the desired curvature.
>
> Such a laborious process required at least one year for the erection of a bridge and the removal of all traces of construction. More time was needed to fill the stone quarry and complete the landscaping, so that the finished product would blend into the scenery as if nature had put it there.[19]

Each of the bridges has the date of completion carved into its surface—a hint of the stories behind them. Only the truly inquisitive visitor will find the inscription, as the date is in a different place on each bridge, but the search provides enticement for examining all aspects of the bridges.

The Gate Houses —Architectural Whimsy

The Jordan Pond and Brown Mountain gate houses constitute the other major architectural statements at Acadia. They were both designed by Grosvenor Atterbury, a prominent New York architect who had designed a handsome barn complex in the style of the eighteenth-century barns of the French nobility for JDR Jr.'s estate in Tarrytown.

Having seen the highly variable styles and uneven quality of

The wooden structural support still in place under the arch of Hemlock Bridge in 1924. *C.P. Simpson personal collection*

park architecture in the West, Rockefeller was determined that any buildings he built at Acadia should be the very best. To develop an appropriate style for Acadia, he arranged for Atterbury to tour the western parks in the fall of 1929 under the aegis of the National Park Service. In his extensive report, Atterbury put forward some principles for determining appropriate styles to use in the future and made his own very candid appraisals of park architecture. One evening at the beginning of his tour, he wrote:

> Sitting on the steps of the Lodge, watching the profile of the Tetons, across Jackson Lake, change from pink to purple in the twilight—one's first guess at the solution of National Park Architecture is that it should begin with the elimination of the cigarette stump and sardine can and end in an Indian 'teepee.'
>
> Any approach to such a sight as we have been watching except it be in quiet and solitude appears sacrilegious. . . .
>
> However you derive it theoretically and stylistically, any Architecture in our National Parks is bound to be, in fact, the physical point of contact, comparison and contrast between the latest handiwork of human civilization and the oldest untouched monuments of Nature. The handiwork of man in the face of the work of God.

At the end of his journey, Atterbury offered five principles to be considered when thinking of style: First, that "undesigned" buildings be kept small and therefore inconspicuous; second, that all buildings be sited "entirely outside the picture," so that they do not compete with the scenery; third, that "ancient local traditions" be used as models for design whenever possible; fourth, that compatible "foreign style" be adapted to serve where indigenous traditions are not available; and fifth, that it is also possible to design along "original or eclectic lines." In conclusion, Atterbury wrote:

> . . . [W]hat we may call the determinants of Architectural style or design do not spring from the human fancy through the pencil of the designer. They have their roots in the premises of the problems given him to solve—in the conditions of climate, the state of the constructional arts, the standards of living and esthetic taste, the human equation, the materials available, the nature of the environment and conditions of all kinds as well as the practical requirements that must be met, by no means forgetting, in this case, the general policy to be followed in the development of the National Parks.[20]

In line with these recommendations, Rockefeller and Atterbury chose a "foreign style" reminiscent of European hunting lodges for the Acadia gate houses. Following Atterbury's principle that structures should not intrude upon the view, both gate houses are located inconspicuously on the edge of the road and surrounded by forest.

In 1913, landscape architect Charles Peterson wrote about them to the director of the National Park Service:

> . . . Mr. Atterbury went on to say that he felt that a very good type of architecture for use in Acadia Park would be this French type which originated in the Romanesque period and which is found in picturesque abundance in certain parts of France. . . . He said he felt that Acadia Park called for a somewhat more sophisticated treatment of architecture and that the French tradition seemed particularly fitting to be carried out in this area because of its early French Colonial association.[21]

George Dorr was pleased when he learned of the recommended French Romanesque architectural style, as it reminded him of the island's early connections with France and particularly of Sieur de Monts, who came from the same region in France where the style originated. Sieur de Monts never actually visited Mount Desert (he remained in Canada while his pilot, Samuel de Champlain, sailed down the coast to Acadia), but he did lay claim to large coastal areas in the name of France. A deep spring near Bar Harbor had already been named after Sieur de Monts by George Dorr, who sometime before 1908 had rescued the spring from development and given it to the park.

Peterson went on to describe the building materials: "These buildings are being built of granite masonry after a local style in the Le Puis district in France. The special characteristic of this type of masonry is that the stone is coursed so that the walls present a banded appearance." The style fits very comfortably into the scene at the edge of the woods and makes an inviting entrance to the carriage roads. The cut stone of the walls is interspersed with bands of handmade brick, and the upper story is half-timbered, with small leaded windows. It all creates a rather whimsical impression. The houses are set in small lawns where the forest reaches close around them.

As well as being engaging to look at, these lodges had a practical function. They were built to mark the entrances to the carriage-road system and to prevent automobiles from entering except for the purposes of park maintenance and fire prevention. A gate was incorporated as part of each structure, and the lodges were to be lived in by park personnel who could monitor the gates.

A third lodge JDR Jr. had planned for his property beside Eagle Lake was never built. Also designed by Atterbury, the immense structure was to be a combination gate lodge, tea house, and "carriage and saddle center" situated on a narrow piece of land

The Jordan Pond Gate House in 1934. *C.P Simpson personal collection*

between the northern shore and the town road. However, Eagle Lake supplied the drinking water for Bar Harbor, and after a great deal of discussion about the sanitary issues involved, the water company declined to issue a permit.

Landscaping Roads with Beatrix Farrand: "Better done than anything I could do."

Whenever JDR Jr. embarked on a project, he sought out professionals to advise him, and he had an unerring instinct for the best. The design of roadside plantings is no exception. In the early 1920s, Beatrix Farrand began working for the Rockefellers to design and build a garden at The Eyrie, in Seal Harbor. Farrand and her husband had a summer home near Bar Harbor, and were as devoted to Mt. Desert as the Rockefellers. Mrs. Farrand's own gardens were known for their beautiful native plantings and an exotic collection of azaleas. A nationally known landscape architect, she worked on many large private estates, such as the Robert Bliss gardens at Dumbarton Oaks in Washington, D.C., and on such college campuses as Yale and Princeton.

As Farrand's work on the gardens at The Eyrie progressed and JDR Jr. grew increasingly confident of her abilities, it was not surprising that he turned to her for help in restoring his roadsides. Before the late 1920s, when he engaged Farrand, JDR Jr. had used the services of Charles Miller, a Seal Harbor nurseryman, for the reforestation and cleanup on the carriage roads. Miller was an able forester and horticulturist, and he continued to work on the roads under Farrand's direction, but he was not a designer, and the roadside work was very demanding. Farrand was clearly a great help to JDR Jr.—as he indicated to her in 1931 after they had been working together for some time:

> I have driven and ridden a number of times since reaching Seal Harbor. This is just a note to tell you how pleased I am with the planting in so far as I have seen it. You cannot know what a relief it is to me to have you giving attention to these matters for it had become quite a burden to me to try to keep up with them on all the roads. Then too, what you do is so much better done than anything I could do. Please accept this renewed assurance of my deep gratitude to you for the very real service you are rendering to the National Park and also to me.[22]

In an earlier letter, he spoke of feeling enough at home with her to share his thoughts regarding park matters beyond planting and landscaping issues:

> I do not know when I have spent an entire half day in so carefree and enjoyable a manner as last Sunday afternoon. I was glad to have the opportunity to talk over with you some of the problems which you are working with in Mrs. Rockefeller's garden. Furthermore, it was a source of genuine satisfaction to have the leisurely chance of thinking out loud with you in regard to certain possible plans for the extension and development of the National Park. . . . I hope I was successful in making clear to you how truly appreciative I am of all that you are doing for the park in improving and developing the various projects which I have roughed out and to which the finishing touches which you are adding mean so much. To feel that I could talk as frankly as I did about park matters, with the perfect assurance that nothing that was said would go further, added much to my satisfaction and sense of freedom in the talk.[23]

In her reply, Farrand expressed similar feelings of confidence and friendship:

> Of course you knew how much pleasure your letter of the 16th of May would give me and therefore took the time and trouble to write it. I too spent an entirely delightful afternoon, as I know of nothing more pleasant than to discuss the things in which one is heart and soul interested with an understanding friend . . . and I enjoyed particularly your thinking out loud as to possible future plans for park matters.[24]

However, given the crowded schedules of both JDR Jr. and Beatrix Farrand, long afternoons working together on the carriage roads were an infrequent pleasure, so they developed their own communication system. Farrand kept extensive and very detailed Road Notes, and she sent them to JDR Jr. on a regular basis. He then would send back his replies. Her notes were a kind of running commentary on the planting progress on the roads — reporting on what had been done to date, suggesting additions or alterations, and making recommendations for new plantings, including varieties of plants and locations (see Appendix C).

Both Farrand and Rockefeller felt that it was important to restore the roadsides to as natural and beautiful a condition as possible. They removed deadfall, restored the topsoil, and used massive quantities of native and naturalized plant materials. Plantings were arranged in irregular patterns to resemble plant habits in the wild, and special care was taken to open up or frame the views.

JDR Jr. had his own clear ideas as to the purpose of the plantings, the effects he had in mind, and the types of plants he wanted—ideas he had been developing and using for years. He seems to have sought a combination of the natural landscape and the hand of humans. He was trying to come close to the beauties of nature while at the same time introducing the orderliness by which humans have attempted to make their seemingly chaotic world comprehensible. Clearly, he regarded beauty and order as inextricably entwined. The infinite care that he, with Beatrix Farrand's help, lavished on the roadside plantings at Acadia provides eloquent testimony to this credo. To make the roads blend into the natural setting, he wanted to use native plant materials as they appeared in the area. As he wrote to Farrand:

> Yesterday I rode to the north of Eagle Lake highway and was greatly pleased with the natural growth which is developing so rapidly along the roadside, also with the planting which I saw in various places. Each year adds to the beauty of these roads as the scars of construction disappear and nature creeps up as close as we will let her to the travelled way of the road.[25]

With equal passion, he wanted the roadsides to be neat and inviting to the human eye, and despite his rigorous habit of humility, he clearly counted himself among those with well-trained eyes. As he said to Horace Albright in a letter about road cleanup at Yellowstone National Park, "The interest which your office and your employees are taking in this road-cleaning work only goes to show that even the untrained eye likes the beautiful and the orderly better than the ugly and the untidy, when an opportunity to compare the two is given."[26]At Acadia it was said that his maintenance men were instructed to keep their eyes out at all times for deadfall along the roads and to remove at once any they found. His correspondence with Farrand includes a telling sequence in which they discuss at some length the relative merits of cutting all the dead limbs off some diseased trees bordering the roads, cutting off only those limbs that are within arm's reach, or leaving the dead branches as they are and waiting to remove the whole tree when it was completely dead. Both he and Farrand agreed that taking off some branches was worse than taking off none, and he finally resolved to leave the dead branches on the trees and only cut out trees that were entirely gone.

Beatrix Farrand understood JDR Jr.'s ideals perfectly, and she intended to carry them out. She worked closely with him, noting his preferences and desires and at the same time giving him the benefit of her own judgment. Using her very perceptive eye and her wide knowledge of native plant materials, she brought to bear her own considerable sensitivity to the particular characteristics of the island in terms of both its physical beauties and its climatic conditions. She observed which plants were prominent in a particular area and then followed this as a guideline for additional planting. When introducing plants, she used each one according to its preferred location. "Spruces and pines grow naturally in this neighborhood," she said of Paradise Hill, "and should be used as the mainstay of the planting, grouping them irregularly." Later, in the same notes: "In the triangle near Half Moon Pond it would be attractive to use hemlock in the plantation as these trees are thriving in the neighborhood and as they are somewhat uncommon it might be well to take the cue given by the trees growing naturally in the neighborhood and make a considerable planting of Hemlock among the small spruces."[27]

Native plants were often taken from one location where they were plentiful to another where there was a bare spot. "It might be advisable to try to get some seed of the native Hornbeam . . . an uncommon tree but charming in its slim growth and adding variety to a plantation," suggested Farrand. She had many other favorites, and in a letter told JDR Jr. about several of them:

> The dwarf scrub oak was also spoken of as interesting to use. . . . This grows in occasional spots on Dog Mountain and might be raised from acorns. Another interesting tree to use occasionally is the Jack Pine. . . . This pine grows vigorously on Schoodic Point and also in a sheltered hollow on the Southeast slope of Green Mountain. It is not a common tree but is interesting botanically and might be worth using in a few groups.[28]

When more plants were needed than they could find in the wild or purchase, Farrand and JDR Jr. had them propagated by the thousands in the Rockefeller nursery under the skillful hand of Charles Miller.

Miller often went with Farrand on her roadside tours to discuss

Beatrix Farrand worked untiringly with JDR Jr. to restore and landscape the surroundings of the later carriage roads. *Dumbarton Oaks Research Library and Collections*

the landscaping and plants. He then took charge of preparing the ground, staking out the plants, and installing them. All of this he seems to have done extraordinarily well, except for the fact that he and his men sometimes had a tendency to plant trees or shrubs in nurserylike rows—a failing that Farrand lamented from time to time in her reports: "... Possibly a small alteration or two may have to be made on the planting of the Aunt Betty's Pond road as I fear some of the tree lines may be over straight, but this can be done with trifling cost and labor. It seems very difficult for Mr. Miller to see that his foremen do not sprinkle the trees primly in an almost unvaryingly straight line."[29]

Farrand was adamant that shrubs or trees be placed in as natural a manner as possible—in clumps of differing size, variety, and height and according to nature's irregular patterns.

Enormous quantities of plants were used, and the work went on during all the later road-building years, including along the carriage roads around Eagle Lake, in the Witch Hole–Paradise Hill area, the Aunt Betty Pond road, and the Bubble Pond–Triad road.

Plantings were used to screen the carriage roads from the motor roads, to separate visually one carriage road from another, to restore the roadside banks after construction was completed, to frame views, and to allow the roads to blend back into the landscape. In a typical selection from her notes, Mrs. Farrand made the following suggestions:

> The bare banks on Paradise Hill, especially on the upper side of the road, should be planted with trees and shrubs, making an occasional plantation of one particular sort of shrub, such as Diervilla, Wild Rose and Sweet fern, as these occur normally in masses and clumps.
>
> Another old road scar near the Paradise Hill road is to be healed by planting.... Try to get creepers started over the bare rocks on the west side of the road. On the opposite side of the road young oaks, pines and Diervilla.
>
> As a good foreground to the bay view use heavy groups of wild rose and Diervilla, and Sweet fern. These will never grow high enough to interfere with the prospect but will make an attractive and clean foreground.
>
> ... The north slope of the hill could be gradually planted with these [pitch pine] giving a splendid Chinese effect to the superb northern prospect. These pitch pine will never intrude on the view any more than they do on the Shore Drive where they add great picturesqueness to the position.[30]

More than sixty varieties of trees, shrubs, and perennials were selected, most native to the island. The rest were primarily plants that had naturalized in the Northeast (see Appendix B). Among the trees Farrand and JDR Jr. chose most frequently were red maples and other hardwoods, such as beech, oak, and the native hornbeam, birch (both paper and yellow), plus several of the native evergreens, such as white pine, pitch pine, spruce, hemlock, and cedar. For smaller trees and shrubs they chose elderberry, winterberry, shad, and dogwood, as well as wild roses, sweet fern, and witch hazel, providing seasonal bloom and fragrance at the woodland edge.

JDR Jr. did not always agree with Farrand's suggestions and did not hesitate to say so. On the other hand, he was the first to admit when he had been won over, as revealed in their correspondence regarding some small native trees: "It was never more beautiful on Mount Desert Island than when I was there over the weekend. I loved it, and for the first time could understand why you are so partial to wild cherries and pear trees. The blossoms certainly are lovely."[31]

A week later Farrand replied: "The Island looked lovely. The cherries were still in bloom and the young birch leaves brilliant. It was nice of you to tell me how much you appreciated my liking for the cherry and shad-bush at this season of the year."[32] Having secured JDR Jr.'s approval, she quickly made a record in her Road Notes: "Mr. Miller was reminded that Mr. Rockefeller now likes the wild cherry (Prunus pennsylvanica) and these may be used wherever they will not interfere with the better tree material."

For special color, Farrand included many annual and perennial wildflowers and vines, such as clematis, honeysuckle, asters, iris, cardinal flower, and waterlilies. For those who enjoyed nibbling as they walked, there were blueberries, huckleberries, and blackberries. All still reward hikers, bikers, riders, and carriage folk who today use the carriage roads.

Large quantities of loam or topsoil were brought in or saved from the road construction to cover old gravel pits and road scars in preparation for planting, and special planting pockets were built in areas where there was little soil. After an area had been planted, Rockefeller, Farrand, and Miller would go back again and again and look it over in different seasons, making adjustments and adding plants. At the same time, they would be discussing plans for their next project. They looked at each road from many vantage points: how it intersected with other roads, what views were important to develop or maintain, where bare spots or unpleasant growth could be corrected. In Farrand's words:

> With this in mind the suggestion is made that possibly next autumn or spring a considerable area now covered with worthless grey birch, lying west and north of the Green Mountain Road and fairly near the entrance to the new mountain road, should be completely cleared of the birches

and replanted in big clumps of pine, bearing in mind that the pine, as they grow, should be grouped so that vistas of the mountains may be attractively placed between the plantations.[33]

JDR Jr. especially liked the long views of mountains or ocean, but he enjoyed close-in views as well. Beatrix Farrand shared this delight, and the Road Notes are full of references to vistas that could be framed by judicious plantings and to places where careful cutting of existing trees was needed to open up a potential vista. The Road Notes for October 1932, for example, stated: "Mr. Rockefeller said he would be glad if Mrs. Farrand and Mr. Miller would take the time this autumn to cut a considerable number of vistas in the roads as mentioned in the notes during the last eighteen months—Paradise Hill, Aunt Betty's Pond, north end of Long Pond, etc."[34]

Charles Miller had a good eye and a good hand himself in this regard, as Farrand was quick to acknowledge in a letter to JDR Jr.:

> . . . You will, I am sure, be interested and thrilled when you see the thinning and vistas which Mr. Miller has cut in the Paradise Hill road. They seem to me to be done with great taste and restraint as one is conscious of a succession of changing vistas separated by groups of fine trees and an infinitely more attractive series of views than would have been the case had Mr. Miller slashed trees and made one panoramic expanse.[35]

Oftentimes, the carriage roads intersected, and sometimes as many as three or four roads came together. At these points, JDR Jr. devised triangles to break up the otherwise overly large areas of gravel. He and Farrand worked with great care to plant these spaces so they would appear to be cutouts from the surrounding woods. Today they are like islands of woodland growth that separate and screen the converging roads from each other and make the junctions appear less like traffic intersections. Here are Farrand's notes for the triangle southwest of Eagle Lake Road:

> In this triangle, tall maples were suggested, combined with small evergreens, if possible. Also shrubs would be attractive so that one road line might be screened from two of the others. This would in no way be unsafe as carriages could easily be seen approaching before they pass behind the screen of the triangle.[36]

In addition to the extensive grading, planning, and planting that she did on the later carriage roads, Farrand worked on the landscaping of the later bridges as well as the two gate houses. In fact, her work gradually expanded until she was reviewing almost all the carriage roads and bridges. She knew where pruning was necessary to maintain views, where additional plantings would be beneficial, and where any other kind of improvement was needed. Even though most of her major plantings in the northern section of the park were destroyed by the Great Fire of 1947, her handiwork remains along the carriage roads elsewhere.

For the Eagle Lake Bridge, the Bubble Pond Bridge, and the Duck Brook Bridge, Farrand recommended plantings that would heal the construction scars and restore the vegetative background and natural setting while always ensuring that the bridge structure would be set off to greatest advantage. As with all the work she did, each year she continued to review and amend what had been done the year before. All through the Road Notes are references to the bridge plantings. She would recommend taking out some plants or adding others to get the effect she and JDR Jr. were seeking. She also was responsible for the design of many of the small bridges on the northern carriage roads. These small, flat structures consisted most often of a stream-spanning concrete slab covered with road gravel and finished with railings made of adze-hewn timbers.

When JDR Jr. specifically asked Farrand to make recommendations for the two gate houses designed by architect Grosvenor Atterbury, he placed these two strong-willed designers in a potentially delicate situation. Atterbury, of course, had his own ideas as to how the landscaping should be done around his buildings, and he felt that Farrand's suggestions included too many cultivated plants, such as the common hydrangea, and that there should be irregular trees in groupings instead of specimen trees as she recommended. When she did not respond to all his requests or answered in a vague manner, being naturally convinced of the value of her own views, he wrote to JDR Jr., barely containing his irritation. Stating precisely what he thought should be done, he described each incident where he felt Farrand had ignored his wishes, and explained why his ideas made more sense than hers. How JDR Jr. smoothed Atterbury's ruffled feathers and resolved the situation is not known, but the subsequent correspondence between himself and Farrand indicates that she continued to do the work. In fact, a terrace in front of the Jordan Pond Gate House was built as she recommended in order to save several trees. She and JDR Jr. also had a lengthy dialogue about a mound that she proposed for one side of the Brown Mountain Gate House to frame the buildings and define the space around them. He felt uneasy about it, and, after carefully studying the situation on the site, he rejected the mound on the grounds that it would impede the view of the lodge from the road.

Beatrix Farrand was a woman of regal bearing and firm opinions—opinions that could have created a personality clash between her and JDR Jr. But fortunately, beyond their obvious mutual love for Mount Desert Island, JDR Jr. and Farrand shared deeply the same views about landscaping the carriage roads. They had so much respect for each other, and they both were so adroit in using the social conventions of the time for polite discourse, that they could negotiate the issues over which they disagreed and enjoy to the full the great work that they did together. In fact, Farrand became so committed to the landscaping and restoration of the carriage roads that she did not charge for her time during at least part of the period she worked with JDR Jr. He was pleased and uneasy at the same time, writing to her:

> I still feel guilty to have you give so much professional attention to these matters without compensation nor would I be comfortable to let the matter stand as it is did I not feel sure you would be perfectly frank with me and tell me without hesitation when you are willing to permit me to recognize this helpful cooperation on the usual professional basis.[37]

But later in the same letter, he added: "Please know that there is no road which I build for which I do not covet your gracious interest and skillful consideration. . . . I should like to feel you would advise about the planting along the sides of any road which I build."

She in turn frequently ended her letters by reiterating her pleasure in working with him and her firm commitment to carrying out his wishes. On May 10, 1932, she wrote: "You would have so much enjoyed seeing the deer, the partridges and the beauty of the spring on the Island and I wished for you constantly on the long drive."[38] And then a week later: "You know without my repeating it how greatly I hope we may meet at our much loved Island. If it is not, however, possible, please let me carry out your wishes in whatever way seems best to you."[39]

Epilogue

Mount Desert Island continues to wield its magic on all who are associated with it. The descendants of the early summer and local residents who worked to make Acadia National Park a reality feel the same deep affection for the place as their forefathers did. So do those who pass through as tourists. My grandfather's descendants come each summer to the island, migrating back like birds to a favorite nesting ground. His grandchildren and now his great grandchildren take the same pleasure in the woods, mountains, and waters of the island as he did. They still use his carriage roads for walking, biking, and picnicking. His son David owns Barr Hill, where The Eyrie used to stand. He and his wife lovingly maintain the gardens on the hill and about seven miles of the carriage roads, including those around Long Pond and Gardiner–Mitchell Hill.

In Seal Harbor and Northeast Harbor, the village improvement societies continue to maintain the local hiking trails in addition to cleaning their beach, maintaining the scenic views from local oceanfront roads, and keeping up the village green. The Northeast Harbor group also produces a map of all the hiking trails and carriage roads on the island. In Bar Harbor, the village association's principal work is to maintain the Shore Path along the northern edge of town fronting Frenchman Bay and to keep the town clock in working order.

The Hancock County Trustees of Public Reservations still exist, but their role has changed. They turned over their remaining lands to the government in the thirties and forties, at the same time as JDR Jr. did, and since then they have functioned primarily as custodians of the historic Black Mansion in Ellsworth and as a social organization. They have one meeting a year at the mansion to socialize over tea.

A new organization, The Friends of Acadia, has arisen to take the Trustees' place as protectors of Mount Desert Island's beauty. Founded in the spirit of JDR Jr. and George Dorr, they work to raise funds for park programs and resources, to encourage volunteer work within the park, and to "increase citizen understanding and appreciation of the Park." Both permanent and summer residents serve on the board of directors. They have chosen as one of their first

135

major projects the establishment of a fund for restoration and maintenance of the carriage roads.

In addition to these formally constituted groups, there are many unknown and unsung individuals who, in simple but important ways, help maintain the park's foot trails and carriage roads. These dedicated folk tend to be those who go into the park regularly. Often they know Acadia's least-frequented spots, and they watch the seasonal changes and the course of nature over the years. They pick up litter as they walk, and they work to keep paths clear of brush; one woman uses her first spring outing each year to gather any debris she finds along the edges of the carriage roads. Another regular visitor has persuaded the park to let him manicure the carriage roads around the Bar Harbor area for cross-country skiers, on his own time and using his own equipment.

The commitment of individual staffers within the Acadia National Park Service has remained high over the years, but the ability of the park to maintain the carriage roads has changed a great deal since 1960, when the park service took over that responsibility after my grandfather's death. While Acadia was being developed, the dedication and drive of Dorr and Rockefeller, plus the prevailing interest in national parks, ensured that funds were available for road repair. However, as time passed, there came to be many more national parks competing for funds from Congress, and there was no longer a great patron to help make up the difference as federal funds were cut.

The park had a maintenance staff of forty people in 1960, and they were responsible for the all of the park, including woodlands, hiking trails, and motor roads. No additional people were hired when carriage-road maintenance was added to their existing responsibilities, and no particular person was assigned to oversee road management. Since that time, funds for maintenance have shrunk steadily, until by the 1980s there were only four permanent maintenance people for the entire park and one person working half-time to care for all the hiking trails and the carriage roads. A few summer interns were hired each year, but it was still an impossible situation.

Within this framework of shrinking budgets and staff, the park has struggled to maintain the carriage roads, but it has been an increasingly difficult task, and the condition of the roads has deteriorated to the point where in some instances they require major work. Coping stones lining the road edges have fallen or been pushed off, especially along the steep mountain slopes. Retaining walls need repointing. Vegetation is clogging the drainage ditches, and the culverts are breaking down. Where heavy grading equipment has been used, it has often removed the crown of the road and pushed dirt and gravel into the drainage ditches. There are signs of erosion everywhere, and many views that were part of the original design have been obscured by trees and brush. Today, Grandfather would not find things to his liking on these beloved roads that he once built and maintained with such lavish care.

It is ironic that the use of the roads has increased and diversified just as the maintenance has deteriorated. Today over eighty percent of all visitors to Acadia National Park walk on the trails and the carriage roads, twenty percent go bicycling, and seven percent take carriage rides or go horseback riding. In addition, there is considerable use by local residents and visitors year-round, for cross-country skiing, dog-sledding, and snowshoeing as well as the summer activities. Some of Grandfather's descendants are reviving the tradition of riding and driving horses on the carriage roads, and park visitors take carriage rides out of the Wildwood Stables near the Jordan Pond Gate House.

The public continues to understand and appreciate the beauties of nature at Acadia, as my grandfather hoped and believed they would. In a letter of appreciation an early visitor expressed sentiments that echoed Grandfather's own: "May I be one, of the proverbial one out of nine, and express my appreciation for the joy and pleasure which I have had in riding over the bridle roads which I am told you are responsible for. These will stand for a long time to come as a monument to community service and to afford opportunity to renew health and strength. At the same time I renewed my inspiration and my touch with Earth and Heaven from the views and vistas."[1]

Perhaps as result of the public devotion to the park and the carriage roads and of a growing environmental awareness and concern in general, the situation is now taking a turn for the better. Superintendent Ronald Wrye managed to have all the stone bridges repointed during his tenure in the mid-1980s, in spite of serious funding shortages. Under the current superintendent, Jack Hauptman, a major study on the carriage roads has been completed with the specific intention of finding a way to restore and care for them again. The park is committed to raising funds from both private and government sources to accomplish this goal. Friends of Acadia is working toward the same end, and new members of the summer community are also joining this endeavor.

Experience has shown that the carriage roads can inspire the interest, enthusiasm, and support that are needed for them to continue. In the view of many people, they fulfill my grandfather's intentions. As one summer resident said, "They seem not only to lead and inspire one's vision, but also one's hopes. They have greatly enriched my spirit—indeed, I have thoroughly enjoyed them."[2] They also make a powerful statement as the personal contribution of a man who is largely known for the extent of his public philanthropic work. In his work on the carriage roads, my grandfather had the opportunity to give of himself. The "Rockefeller roads" are a work worth remembering and preserving in part because they are a demonstration of his skill as a designer and road builder. His innermost sensibilities about nature and spirit were manifested through these skills; he set aside his shyness to reveal what meant most to him in order to share it with other people. The carriage roads became the signature of my grandfather's inner delight made visible on the land he loved.

In this time when the earth is so ravaged as the result of human greed and desire, what better gift could a man of these sensibilities have made?

Appendixes

APPENDIX A:
The Major Bridges of the Carriage-Road System

Designed by Welles Bosworth
>   Cobblestone Bridge (1917)
>   Little Harbor Brook Bridge (1919)
>   Jordan Stream Bridge (1920)
>   Hemlock Bridge (1924)
>   Deer Brook Bridge (1925)—double arch
>   Waterfall Bridge (1925)
>   Chasm Brook Bridge (1926)
>   Hadlock Brook Bridge (1926)

Designed by Charles Stoughton
>   Duck Brook Bridge (1929)—triple arch
>   Amphitheater Bridge (1931)
>   West Branch Bridge (1931)
>   Cliffside Bridge (1932)
>   Jordan Pond–Seal Harbor Bridge (1932)
>   Stanley Brook Bridge (1933)—triple arch

Designed and built by Acadia National Park
>   Triad–Day Mountain Bridge (1940)

APPENDIX B:
Plant List for the Carriage Roads at Acadia National Park (From Beatrix Farrand's "Road Notes")

Trees

Acer ginnala (Japan)	Japanese Maple [Amur Maple]
Acer pensylvanicum	Moosewood
Acer rubrum	Red Maple
Acer spicatum	Mountain Maple
Amelanchier canadensis	Shadblow or Downy Serviceberry [Wild Plum]
Betula alleghaniensis	Yellow Birch
Betula papyrifera	Canoe Birch or White Birch
Betula populifolia	Gray Birch
Cornus alternifolia	Alternate Leaved Dogwood
Cornus sericea	Red Osier Dogwood
Corylus rostrata	Hazel [Beaked Hazel]
Fagus sp.	Beech
Fraxinus americana	White Ash
Fraxinus excelsior	European Ash
Hamamelis virginiana	Witch-hazel
Juniperus virginiana	Cedar [Eastern Red-cedar]
Ostrya virginiana	Hop-hornbeam
Picea sp.	Spruces
Picea abies	Norway Spruce
Pinus sp.	Pines
Pinus banksiana v. divaricata	Jack Pine
Pinus resinosa	Red Pine
Pinus strobus	Eastern White Pine
Pinus sylvestris	Scotch Pine
Pinus virginiana	Virginia Scrub Pine [Virginia Pine; Scrub Pine]
Prunus virginiana	Choke Cherry
Quercus ilicifolia	Dwarf Scrub Oak [Scrub Oak; Bear Oak]
Sorbus aucuparia	Mountain Ash [European Mountain Ash]
Thuja occidentalis	American Arborvitae

Shrubs

Berberis thunbergii	Japanese Barberry
Berberis vulgaris	Common Barberry
Chamaedaphne cassandra [*C. calyculata*]	Leatherleaf [Cassandra]
Gaylussacia brachycera	Huckleberry [Box-huckleberry]
Ilex verticillata	Winterberry
Myrica gale	Sweetgale
Myrica pensylvanica v. carolinensis	Bayberry
Nemopanthus mucronata	Mountain-holly

Rhododendron sp.	Azaleas
Rhus sp.	Sumac
Rhus typhina	Staghorn Sumac
Rosa cinnamomea	Cinnamon Rose [European Cinnamon Rose]
Rosa rubiginosa [*R. eglanteria*]	Sweetbrier Rose [European Sweetbrier Rose]
Sambucus canadensis	Black-berried Elderberry [American Elder]
Sambucus racemosa [*S. pubens?*]	Red-berried Elder
Taxus canadensis	Canada Yew
Vaccinium corymbosum	Highbush Blueberry
Viburnum alnifolium (*V. lantanoides*)	Hobblebush
Viburnum cassinoides	Dewberries [Withe-rod]
Viburnum trilobum	Highbush Cranberry [American Cranberry-bush]
Zenobia pulverulenta	Dusty Zenobia

Perennials: Including Ferns, Flowers, and Vines

Ampelopsis quinquefolia [*Parthenocissus quinquefolia*]	Ampelopsis [Virginia Creeper]
Aster sp.	Asters
[*Rubus* sp.]	Blackberries
Calla palustris	Northern Calla [Water-arum]
Caltha palustris	Marsh Marigold [Cowslip]
Carex morrowii	Sedge [Morrow's Sedge]
Celastrus scandens	Bittersweet [American Bittersweet
Chelone glabra	Turtle-head [White Turtle-head]
Clematis verticillaris	Purple Virgin's Bower [Purple Clematis; Rock Clematis]
Clematis virginiana	Virgin's Bower
Comptonia asplenifolia [*C. peregrina*]	Sweetfern
Convolvulus sepium [*C. mauritanicus?*]	Ground Morning-glory
Eupatorium purpureum	Joe-Pye-Weed [Bluestem Joe-Pye-Weed)
Fern sp.	Ferns
Grass sp.	Grasses
Iris versicolor	Blue Flag Iris
Lilium canadense	Meadow Lily [Canada Lily]
Lilium philadelphicum	Wood Lily
Lilium superbum	Turkscap Lily
Lobelia cardinalis	Cardinal-flower
Lonicera sp.	Honeysuckle
Nymphaea odorata	Water-lily
Rosa palustris	Swamp Rose
Rosa rugosa [naturalized]	Wild Rose [Rugosa Rose]

Sagittaria latifolia	Arrowleaf [Arrowhead]
Solidago sp.	Goldenrod
Thalictrum polygamum	Tall Meadow-rue

Notes: All plants are native to the northeastern United States unless noted, and are listed as found in Beatrix Farrand's Road Notes. Where today's Latin or common names differ from what she used, they are given in brackets.

APPENDIX C:
Excerpts from Beatrix Farrand's Road Notes, 1929 and 1931

[These excerpts from her 1929 Road Notes illustrate the care and imagination with which Mrs. Farrand planned the roadside plantings with JDR Jr. and Charles Miller.]

October 2, 1929

SURROUNDINGS TO NEW DUCK BROOK BRIDGE:

Use small spruces and pines as may be advisable to thin from the evergreen nursery, on the lower parts of the banks North and South of the stream. These little trees may be planted quite thickly and later thinned out where necesary. A few taller trees may be planted near the bridge, deciduous in type. These should be set out as close as possible to the bridge walls and at the extreme ends of the abutments in order not to hide the view of the arches as seen from the adjoining roads. On the East side of the bridge, as the archways do not show very distinctly from the new Eagle Lake road, the trees may be planted closer to the bridge abutments, especially the surroundings to frame the steps on the Southeast end of the bridge. If there be soil enough, a few pines may be planted below the cedar group on the North side of the stream West of the bridge. Shrubs may be planted under the steps and alongside the step wall, and may be planted out to the Eagle Lake road line where they will not make an unsafe screen. Probably some of the large pines Southwest of the bridge will need replacement and further small pines might be added to this group. . . .

NEAR BREAKNECK POND:

Where the old Breakneck road and the new road are unpleasantly visible, it would be well to add to the screen such trees as red maple and birches as well as the small evergreen thinnings, using the evergreen thinnings also on the new road banks near the Breakneck Pond.

It might be advisable to try to get some seed of the native Hornbeam (ostrya virginiana) an uncommon tree but charming in its slim growth and adding variety to a plantation. The dwarf scrub oak was also spoken of as interesting to use (quercus ilicifolia). This grows in occasional spots on Dog Mountain and might be raised from acorns. Another interesting tree to use occasionally is the Jack Pine (pinus divaricata). This pine grows vigorously on Schoodic Point and also in a sheltered hollow on the Southeast slope of Green Mountain. It is not a common tree but is interesting botanically and might be worth using in a few groups. . . .

[Discussion of Various Plants:]

. . . In speaking of various roses to use for the roadside planting the question was raised as to whether rosa rubiginosa (the sweetbriar) were an American or European rose. After investigation this was found to be a European specimen which had been naturalized around the old houses throughout the New England states. It is therefore entirely appropriate to use where a clearing implies an old house and would be particularly attractive near Long Pond, possibly a few on the West side of the road at the

Southeast end of the pond and possibly a few more where the old house used to stand and near its neighboring plantation of apple trees and cinnamon roses.

Another small tree attractive in its flower and much liked by the birds is the chokecherry (prunus virginiana). This makes thickets 5 to 6 feet high, punctuated by trees 15 feet high or more. The black berries are eaten as greedily by the birds as the seed of the red berried elder. . . .

BETWEEN THE MOTOR AND THE BUBBLE POND AND TRIAD ROAD:

More planting is needed to screen one road from the other road. This was the point mentioned specifically by Mr. Rockefeller. Here the mountain maple (acer spicatum), a yellow birch, cedar and ash and red maple would work in well with the surrounding growth. Moosewood also is growing in the neighborhood and could be used if thought advisable.

BEAVER POOL:

. . . Few shrubs should be planted here in order to keep the low swalelike effect opening into the Beaver Pool. Goldenrod and iris would be attractive in this position, also in the meadow on the West side of the road. Iris in groups planted by the stream and occasionally at the pool edges, with an occasional group of black or red elder (not too closely planted) would add modeling to the already prettily graded meadow. At the pool below the culvert winterberry and red berried elder, with possibly a few black berried elder, would overhang the water and appear at home. On the far side of the Beaver Pool a plantation was to be tried of cardinal flower (lobelia cardinalis) where this will be comparatively inaccessible. It would also be pleasant to try turtlehead (chelone glabra), Jo Pye weed (eupatorium purpureum) and meadow rue (thalictrum polygamum), also possibly the swamp rose (rosa carolina) as this gives the opportunity to use this rose in its natural habitat. Myrica gale (sweet gale) would probably grow well on the banks of the Beaver Pool even though it were considerably flooded in spring. An old track shows rather unpleasantly from the present Beaver Pool road, Mr. Miller suggested digging a few holes in the old road in which trees might be planted. These he felt should be $1^1/2'$ deep and 8' to 11' wide and filled with loam. He also suggested that a foot of loam was advisable to cover the rock pile on the North end of the Beaver Pool and that possibly another foot of loam would be needed on the mound built into the north end of the pool. . . .

[During a 1931 visit, Mrs. Farrand checked on the progress of the earlier plantings. Excerpts from her follow-up notes show how thoroughly she monitored all the details of the landscaping.]

October 5, 1931

During a drive around the roads Mr. Miller mentioned to Mrs. Farrand that he was quite concerned as to the condition of the pines on the Barr Hill Road, as many of these showed a considerable blister rust. In fact, Mr. Miller, although not directly authorized to do so by Mr. Rockefeller, had cleaned about 500 trees of patches of rust and would like to know from Mr. Rockefeller whether he should do any further pruning in this neighborhood. Mrs. Farrand thought the pruning would be advisable as the pines are particularly fine in this section.

The holes for planting at the Duck Brook bridge were looked at by Mr. Miller and Mrs. Farrand. Good pockets for planting have been made near the foot of the steps leading from the lower to the upper level on the west side of the bridge, and further pockets have been contrived so that part of the great granite wall of the west side of the bridge will be framed in verdure.

Mr. Miller reported that preparation for a considerable number of holes had already been made in the Paradise Hill section and felt that he did not want to plant too recklessly until after the whole road planting scheme had been reviewed with Mrs. Farrand as he did not wish to exhaust the pines in the nursery for one planting district . . .

Mr. Miller is under the impression that Mr. Rockefeller does not wish to have any dead branches pruned from the trees in this section, but that dead trees are to be taken out, and Mr. Ralston is to be asked to take out only lying dead wood. If the standing dead wood is taken out by Mr. Ralston, Mr. Miller is obliged to seek kindling for his burning outside the forestry area. This matter is to be spoken of with Mr. Ralston. . . .

Mr. Rockefeller was to be asked whether some of the banks on the Aunt Betty's Pond road might not be made slightly less convex in their curves. A note was further made to ask Mr. Ralston whether it would be possible for Mr. Miller and the garden and planters in general to have at any rate some of the muck being taken from the gate lodge cellar near Jordan Pond. . . .

A Knob between the road at Aunt Betty's Pond and the pond edge might be planted with pine and spruce, dividing the view of the pond into two or three large vistas.

An old swamp south of Aunt Betty's Pond might be slightly opened by cutting. No great change is needed here as the charm of the scene is its undisturbed quietude. . . .

It was also noticed how particularly charming the narrow winding road was leading over its many bridges and up through the hardwoods. The bridges simple and pleasant, the soil remarkably fertile and rich and the surrounding wood in apparently excellent condition.

A note was also taken to thicken heavily the plantation between the Y, the Sargent Mountain road, the West Eagle Lake road, and the new bridle path, as these roads are now unpleasantly open to each other.

It was thought that occasional tree cutting might be done to break up the stiff planted spruce lines on the West side of Eagle Lake. This was agreed to by Mr. Miller.

An inspection was made of the Beaver Pool and its planting. Mr. Miller and Mrs. Farrand were glad to see that elders were taking hold here on the east side of the pool and that myriads of Boneset plants were springing up west of the road and that some of the other plants, such as Pontederia and Sagittaria were starting to grow with apparent enjoyment.

It was also mentioned that the rushes might be pulled out of the low sections of the pool where they seemed likely to spread unduly and cover the water surface.

Grading has been done with great success west of the motor road and northeast of Jordan Pond where an ugly bank is now well covered with good soil. This bank has had seven or eight gutters installed in it which seem, Mr. Miller thinks, sufficient to prevent the spring freshets from washing the top soil off. Mr. Miller suggested, and Mrs. Farrand enthusiastically agreed, in planting good sized red berried elders (Sambucus racemosa) close to these gutters where the shrubs will soon spread and cover over the necessary but not ornamental gutters.

APPENDIX D:
**Excerpt from *The Future of Mount Desert Island:
A Report to the Plan Committee, Bar Harbor
Village Improvement Association,*
by Charles W. Eliot 2nd, 1928**

Horse Carriage Roads

The extensive system of carriage roads constructed by Mr. John D. Rockefeller, Jr., and open to the public on horseback or in horse-drawn vehicles, whether on his private property or in the park, constitutes a second means of recreational enjoyment of the Island. The more leisurely speed of movement, the narrower right of way and the sharper curvature of the road make this method of access more suited to intimate enjoyment of beauty with less destruction than in the case of automobile roads.

The horse roads already constructed form a rather complicated system in the southern part of the Island with more extensive branches around Sargent Mountain and north to the Eagle Lake Road. The use of these roads appears to be growing, but as yet is very slight. The inauguration last summer of a buckboard service is an encouraging sign of a possible increased use and of the development of the kind of activity which might be made a distinctive feature of the Park and Island. Just as in Cornwall, England, the thing to do is to go on a tally-ho, so some day at Mount Desert the buckboard may regain its former popularity.

The offer of Mr. Rockefeller to build more carriage roads in the vicinity of the Witch Hole, through the Bubble Pond Valley, and around the head of Eagle Lake has aroused anew questions as to the desirable extent of the carriage road system in relation to the foot trail system and the wilderness areas.

The arguments in favor of more carriage roads are briefly these: (1) The roads make it possible for those who cannot or will not walk to see and enjoy a greater number and variety of the scenic beauties of the Island. (2) The roads are useful in the administration of the Park to control fire and poaching. (3) The roads, being open only to horses, horse-drawn vehicles and pedestrians, may encourage riding and driving in contrast to motoring. (4) The work involved in construction of more roads means employment during the slack season for large numbers of persons on the Island. (5) The National Park Service considers itself morally bound to Mr. Rockefeller, to whom the Park is indebted for the motor road, to continue the construction of those horse-carriage roads which were approved by the Park Service in 1924 when the motor road was under discussion.

The arguments against more carriage roads are usually directed against specific projects but are based on the following theories: (1) That a carriage road, as a man-made object, destroys the wilderness character or solitude of the area through which it is constructed. (2) That the scars already made on the mountain sides will not cover for a generation and that no more should be added. (3) That a carriage road to the same point or along the same route as a foot trail mitigates the pleasure of walking because it destroys one of the reasons for walking,—to reach a point now otherwise inaccessible. It is contended that since walking is admittedly the best way to see and enjoy the Island, nothing should be done to discourage the walker.

(4) That the very slight use of the existing carriage roads indicates no need of further construction at least until the value and usefulness of the existing roads are proven. (5) That although built for horse-drawn vehicles, the carriage roads are potential motor roads and that motoring on these roads would be not only dangerous to the motorist but destructive to the scenic values. (6) That the construction of too many roads will destroy the "scale" of the Island and Park; that the mountains are low though bold, and that a road by which you can quickly pass from end to end or ascend their heights will reduce, as a measuring stick, their apparent size. (7) Finally the opponents of more roads quote from the "Official Policy Governing National Parks" previously referred to, and which includes a statement that "the over-development of parks and monuments by the construction of roads should be zealously guarded against."

A basis for a general plan has been suggested which, if adopted by the Park Service, would safeguard "Wilderness Areas" and allow a small amount of additional road construction in connection with "Centers."

APPENDIX E:
Letter from Frederick Law Olmsted, Jr., to JDR Jr.

Eureka, California,
July 11th, 1930.

Mr. J.D. Rockefeller, Jr.,
26 Broadway,
New York, New York.

Dear Sir:

I beg to submit the following report in regard to certain proposed horse-and-carriage roads on the Island of Mt. Desert, planned by your engineers but all reviewed on the ground by me and in a few places relocated in accordance with suggestions by me.

These roads cannot be considered intelligently except in the light of a reasonable conception of the purposes and desirable future condition not only of these roads but of other parts of the system of such horse roads which you have had under construction for many years past. My conception, which I believe to be substantially in harmony with your own, is that in appearance the roads should ultimately take on much of the aspect of some of the old wood-roads untraversed by motor vehicles, wheel tracks and hoof marks on a sylvan ribbon of grass and low ground cover, although kept free from excessive encroachment of underbrush and systematically made easier, safer, and pleasanter for driving on with horse-drawn vehicles and even for riding on horseback than is apt to be the case with old logging roads in rough topography. Some of the older of the roads of the system built for you have already attained or closely approached this ideal, but many of them as yet fall short of it in appearance, partly because of certain details of construction or maintenance which I believe could be improved upon, but mainly because they are yet too new and especially because they have been subjected and are now being subjected to a very considerable use by automobiles.

Their use by automobiles is mainly of two sorts, both very difficult to control in such a way as to permit the desired adaptation of the roads to their proper purposes. One of these is the use of the roads, after their completion, by trucks engaged in repairs and in the construction of other roads and in forestry work and by automobiles carrying men engaged in such continuing work. The other is the unauthorized, indeed the strictly forbidden, use of the roads by the automobiles of those who find sufficient convenience or pleasure in using them to disregard the prohibition. The latter use is reported to be, and very apparently is, extensive.

I am convinced that satisfactory progress in adapting these "horse-roads" to their proper function, and in bringing them to an appearance thoroughly suitable for that function, can be made only if these two difficulties are dealt with systematically and adequately.

I believe this involves two things which are troublesome but must be squarely faced. On the one hand it means that, in general, so far as it is necessary for vehicles to continue to traverse these roads for repairs or construction work or forestry work, horse drawn vehicles must be provided and maintained for such work, including, where necessary, horse drawn "barges" or stages for the transportation of workmen; probably supplemented, where distances are great, by the definite assignment of one or more pieces of road as definite "service roads", permanently intended for use by motorized work cars, leading in from a public highway to a distributing terminal point beyond which it will be physically impossible for motors to pass, and physically shut off from connection with the horse-roads proper. On the other hand it means that the system of horse-roads proper must be made impassable for unauthorized motor cars. They can obviously be made inaccessible to motor cars except at a limited number of points. Each of these points can be controlled, and should be controlled, in either one of two ways: One is an ordinary gate with an attendant constantly on watch, except when it is locked for the night or the season; simple, but involving a large labor cost. The other is a special type of barrier, impassable by any ordinary automobile with its very low clearance between the wheels but readily passable by horses and by any ordinary types of horse drawn vehicles, which have much higher clearances under the axles. Some experimenting may be necessary to develop the right type of barrier, but I am quite sure it can be done because I have several times encountered roads, readily passable by horse drawn vehicles, which because of the deepness of the wheel tracks below the tops of intervening obstacles could not be negotiated by an automobile without several hours labor on a stretch of a comparatively few feet.

Assuming then, some such complete and effective exclusion of motor cars from the "horse-road" system proper, the horse roads can, without serious difficulty, be made to serve very delightfully three purposes of large aggregate importance in an area like that of the Acadia National Park and similar adjacent lands: (1) driving in horse drawn vehicles in narrow, winding woodland roads in varied and beautiful scenery, completely free from the annoyance and even the dread of meeting motor cars[,] a pleasure so real and so extraordinarily rare today that systematic provision for it with opportunity provided for people to hire the horses and rigs may reasonably be expected to develop into one of the most unique attractions of the Park and of the Island; (2) horseback riding on safe routes of easy gradients supplementing a system of narrow and often steep horse trails to places more difficult of access, an attraction less unique but of large and growing importance; (3) walking on pleasant routes of easy gradient as a supplement to the paths intended exclusively for pedestrians available at least until such time as the use of the roads by carriages and horses may become too great for their use by pedestrians as well.

For these purposes it is desirable to keep the gradient of these ways, except as an occasional very short steep pitch may be desirable in fitting them to the topography, not exceeding a maximum of five per cent. The alignment may be as irregular and occasionally within certain limits as abrupt, as topographic irregularities suggest. Indeed, it is perhaps a fair criticism of some of the "horse-roads" built for you in the past that the smoothness of the curvature is in some places rather too suggestive of a motor-road, or of the rather sophisticated and smooth-flowing roads which landscape architects and engineers were wont to build in city parks and private estates in the days before the automobile, rather than of the pleasantly accidental-seeming yet thoroughly practicable and convenient woods-roads which one associates with wild areas [such as] these. As to width, I believe it unlikely that the numbers of carriages using these roads will be so great that it will be necessary to provide uniformly, and throughout their entire length under all topographic conditions, the full width of sixteen feet necessary for two carriages to pass easily without slowing up. Indeed, as already stated, I conceive these roads as showing, in the main, when they have become mellowed with time, a single pair of wheel tracks, out of which meeting carriages would turn on the herbage of the "shoulders" in order to pass each other. And where heavy grading would be required to make the full width of sixteen feet traversable on the occasion of such meetings I should not hesitate to reduce the width of the graded roadbed[,] merely taking care to provide "turn-outs" ample for safe passing with sufficient frequency and so related to any bends in the road that there would always be a good passing place ahead of both drivers when they come in sight of each other.

It is with such ideas as the above in mind that I have examined and approved the locations for the horse roads now in question.

The most important of these is a unit leading from the proposed center for riding and driving activities at the north end of Eagle Lake toward Bar Harbor and past Great Meadow. It climbs to the north shoulder of Great Pond Hill on a fairly direct line, through pleasant scenery and on good grades, passing under the present park motor road. Thence it descends through the woods on a five percent grade to Kebo Brook, follows close to the brook until it approaches the open land of the Golf Course, and then runs easterly, just well within the woods. At the north point of Kebo Mountain it is for a short distance rather closely approached by the proposed motor road, but remains below and north of it and pretty well screened from it. One branch leads eastward to the Harden Farm Road a short distance south of Cromwell Harbor Road and just north of the Cemetery. This branch will be useful chiefly to those going between Bar Harbor and the Eagle Lake region on horse back or by horse-drawn carriages. The other branch turns south, to the west of the Cemetery, and then southwest, crossing the little ravine north of Red Rock Spring on a bridge under which the park motor road will also pass. From there the horse road swings across the northeast corner of the open grassland commanding the fine views toward Gorge and Champlain Mountain and Great Meadow Hill, and follows just within the edge of the woods west of that grassland to enter the present Hemlock Road at the northern end of the hemlocks. It is proposed to use that road just as it is through the hemlocks, obliterating its present northern connection across the swampy land to the Harden Farm Road and closing it to automobiles. It is a very beautiful road, admirabl[y] adapted to use by horses but dangerously narrow and crooked for automobiles, and its charm would be lost if it were widened and made safe for automobiles. A short distance north of the Sieur de Monts Spring, after passing the hemlocks, it is proposed to discontinue the present road[,] using its line for a path from a suitable hitching place to the Spring, and to carry the horse road eastward, to the north of the Spring area, mainly on lines already cleared, with a connection across the park motor road and the public highway into the existing horse trails in the Robin Hood Park area of the National Park.

The horse road unit above described will serve to connect the entire system of horse-roads radiating from Eagle Lake pleasantly and easily and directly with the vicinity of Bar Harbor, and with the Great Meadow and Sieur de Monts Spring region and the horse trails in the eastern lobe of the National Park; it will traverse some very beautiful characteristic and varied scenery, and it will not have any appreciable effect upon that scenery.

The second unit is suggested in order to make possible an alternative route between Eagle Lake and Red Rock Spring, longer and involving much more climbing than the first, but offering certain impressive views that cannot be obtained from that or any other horse road, especially the sweeping northwestward and northeastward views from high upon the shoulders of Great Pond Hill. This is done by rising up to and crossing under the present park motor road at a point between the branch motor road to the summit of Cadillac Mountain and the new park motor road which is proposed to be built around the north end of Great Pond Hill to the Great Meadow. It would keep well above the latter and well separated from it but commanding similar distant views before descending into the woods on the east slope of Great Pond Hill. By a short rise it would pass over the saddle between Kebo Mountain and the Flying Squadron and thence descend northeasterly to join the first unit a little to the northwest of Red Rock Spring. I had some misgivings at first as to whether the last mentioned portion of this road might not make a scar on the east face of Kebo Mountain objectionably visible from the Great Meadow side, but I found upon study that this danger is avoidable, and that the whole project is a desirable one, although less important than the first unit. [Olmsted's first two "units" described above were the proposed Kebo Valley roads, which were never built.]

The third horse-road unit is one that was proposed several years ago but was set aside because of opposition which then developed to it. It lies mainly within the Amphitheatre. I have carefully examined all that part of its course and more cursorily the short connection from the point where it leaves the Amphitheatre valley (below the cliffs on the south ridge of Jordan Mountain) to the horse-road southwest of Jordan Pond. It would afford in itself a beautiful ride and drive, distinctive, among other things, for traversing the upper edge of a nearly pure stand of yellow birch on the lower western side of the Amphitheatre, very impressive from within at the season when I saw it, and also for overlooking from among the thinner and smaller growth on the east side of the valley both the widespread foliage canopy of the Amphitheatre and the seaward views to the south. It would also afford a shorter connection than at present and on much easier grades between the horse roads east and west of the Jordan Mountain and Sargent Mountain mass. If the construction of such a road would mar or disturb the great unbroken sweep of sylvan landscape which the Amphitheatre now presents as seen from many points around it I should, notwithstanding these advantages, definitely oppose its introduction; but I satisfied myself that with reasonable care in managing the details of construction no such deplorable result would occur. I believe, therefore, that sooner or later a horse road of the type I have discussed ought to be built here.

Respectfully submitted,
Frederick Law Olmsted

(From the Rockefeller Archive Center collection.)

APPENDIX F:
Letter from JDR Jr. to
Secretary of the Interior Harold L. Ickes

Room 5600
30 Rockefeller Plaza,
New York.

March 14, 1935.

My dear Mr. Secretary:

When Acadia National Park was established, it consisted only of mountain tops bought earlier by interested summer and winter residents of Mount Desert Island as a protection against exploitation for cheap amusement purposes and held in a corporation known as the Hancock County Trustees of Public Reservations until they were turned over to the government. Thus the Park area at the outset was not accessible to any highway and was traversed only by foot trails. Believing that it should ultimately extend to the ocean on one side and to Frenchmans Bay on the other and that access to it would be desirable not only for pedestrians, but, in carefully chosen areas, for lovers of horses as well as automobilists, I began years ago buying lands on the Island, having in mind to make possible the rounding out of the Park boundaries and its extension and development as above outlined.

Since that time I have built many miles of roads on the lands which I own and on the Park lands adjacent thereto, in the latter instance with proper Government approval and consent and without obligation to the Park. Other roads both for motors and for horses have been approved by the Government and are only awaiting public or private funds for their construction. There are still others which I have laid out but which have not yet been officially brought to the attention of the National Park Service or made a part of its park development program. All of these roads have been planned and the lands necessary therefor acquired, in cooperation with the National Park Service and with the general knowledge of the successive Secretaries of the Interior. Many of them have been studied and passed on by Mr. Frederick Law Olmsted, the landscape architect.

Now that all the lands necessary to make possible the above development program have been acquired I am making the following proposal. If after careful review and approval by your Department you should be disposed to include these roads, which have been planned but not yet built, in the official program for the development of Acadia National Park with the understanding that they would be built as opportunity offered and as funds, either public or private, could be made available, I am prepared to deed to the Government for inclusion in Acadia National Park all of the remaining lands which I have acquired for that purpose. This would include (1) lands making possible the extension of the present Park Motor Road across the Eagle Lake Road, to the high bluffs overlooking Frenchmans Bay with a Bar Harbor Park entrance on Eden Street at the site formerly occupied by Mrs. Henderson's house, also a horse road entering at the same place and connecting with the existing horse roads in that area; (2) the right of way of a motor road which I am now building and will complete, from the highway at Seal Harbor by the sea through the Stanley Brook valley and connecting with the present Park Motor Road at the Jordan Pond Road; (3) the Jordan Pond Gate Lodge, the existing Jordan Pond Tea House and the land surrounding them; (4) the Eagle Lake Tea House and Horse Center site at the north end of Eagle Lake.

In brief, the lands which I am prepared to deed to the Government would make possible (1) a Park motor road from the sea on the south at Seal Harbor to Frenchmans Bay on the north at Bar Harbor, connecting with the present Park Motor Road that goes to the top of Cadillac Mountain; also a connection with the Ocean Drive,—including an entrance by the sea at the Homans place—then continuing around Otter Cliffs to the old Radio Station, across Otter Creek inlet, around the Black Woods and back to Jordan Pond. Of this connection I have built the Ocean Drive and am now building the Otter Cliffs and Radio Station section; (2) a horse road Park entrance on Eden Street in Bar Harbor to connect with the existing horse road system in that area; (3) a horse road from Eagle Lake to the Sieur de Monts Spring area and the high hill to the north, returning to Eagle Lake by a different route.

The estimate which my engineers have made of the cost of all of the above roads which either the Park or I am not already building is $1,854,125. This is only a very rough figure. At the same time it gives some idea of what the program might involve. It does not include anything for roadside cleaning, forestry or planting, which would bring the total easily to $2,000,000.

For your information may I add that I have heretofore given to the Park something over 2700 acres of land that cost me over $250,000. For buildings, roads, bridges, forestry and planting on those lands I have spent an additional $500,000. The lands that I am now prepared to give total 3835 acres and cost me over $600,000. For their development with roads and the usual other improvements I have already spent at least $500,000. In addition I have spent for roads built on Park lands roughly $2,000,000. My total expenditure on the project is therefore some $4,000,000.

The map which I am enclosing will show at a glance the facts set forth in the above letter.

                              Very sincerely,
                              John D. Rockefeller, Jr.

(From Acadia National Park Service files.)

Chapter Notes

The following abbreviations have been used throughout these notes: RAC—Rockefeller Archive Center, Tarrytown, New York; SHL—Seal Harbor Library, Mount Desert Island, Maine; NPS—National Park Service, Washington, D.C.

Introduction

1. Horace M. Albright, Diaries. Personal collection of Marion Schenk, Studio City, California.

Chapter 1. The Making of a Landscape Artist

1. Raymond B. Fosdick, *John D. Rockefeller, Jr., A Portrait* (New York: Harper & Brothers, 1956), 188.
2. John D. Rockefeller, Jr., "Remarks on the occasion of the Fiftieth Anniversary of the founding of the Men's Bible Class of the Riverside Church," Commodore Hotel, New York City, February 29, 1944. RAC.
3. Grace Goulder, *John D. Rockefeller: The Cleveland Years* (Cleveland: The Western Reserve Historical Society, 1972), 19.
4. Ibid.
5. A.D. Taylor, *Forest Hill Park—A Report on the Proposed Landscape Development* (Cleveland: Caxton Co., 1938), 20.
6. Ibid.
7. A.J. Downing, *A Treatise on the Theory and Practice of Landscape Gardening Adapted to North America* (New York: Riker, Thorne & Co., 1854 edition), 45.
8. William O. Ingliss, "In Happiness & In Sorrow," unpublished manuscript, Chapter 39, 667, RAC.
9. Fosdick, 8–10.
10. John D. Rockefeller, *Random Reminiscences of Men and Events,* Laurance S. Rockefeller, ed. (Tarrytown, New York: Sleepy Hollow Press, 1984), 38–39.
11. Ibid., 34–37.
12. JDR Jr., Speech at lunch hosted by Harold Swift, Chicago, 9/25/42. RAC.
13. JDR Jr., Remarks at preview of Sunnyside (home of Washington Irving), 10/4/47. RAC.
14. Fosdick, 188.
15. Ibid., 8.
16. Frederick L. Olmsted, Jr., and Theodora Kimball, eds., *Frederick Law Olm-*

sted—*Landscape Architect 1822–1903* (New York: Benjamin Blom, Inc., 1970), 27.

17. Fosdick, 95.

18. *New York Evening Journal,* 11/26/13. RAC.

19. Anonymous; no date or name on article in RAC files.

20. Fosdick, 95.

21. *Albany Times Union,* 1/20/17. RAC.

22. JDR Jr., Speech at opening of Fort Tryon Park, New York City, 10/12/35. RAC.

23. Tom Pyle, *Pocantico—Fifty Years on the Rockefeller Domain* (New York: Duell, Sloan and Pearce, 1964), 100.

24. JDR Jr., Letter to Horace M. Albright, 10/10/33. RAC.

Chapter 2. The Inspiration of the Place

1. Sargent F. Collier, *Mt. Desert Island and Acadia National Park: An Informal History* (Camden, Maine: Down East Books, 1978), ix–x.

2. Samuel Eliot Morison, *The Story of Mount Desert Island* (Boston: Little, Brown, 1960), 3.

3. Collier, 4.

4. *Rules and Regulations: Lafayette National Park,* National Park Service Publication (Washington: U.S. Government Printing Office, 1921), 9.

5. Morison, 49.

6. Richard Walden Hale, Jr., *The Story of Bar Harbor* (New York: Ives Washburn, Inc., 1949), 195.

7. Great Harbor Collection, Museum Archives, Northeast Harbor, Maine.

8. George B. Dorr, *The Story of Acadia National Park* (Bar Harbor, Maine: Acadia Publishing Co., 1942), Book II, 76.

9. Collier, 137.

10. Dorr, Book I, 5–6.

11. George L. Stebbins, "Random Notes on the Early History and Development as a Summer Resort of Mount Desert and Particularly Seal Harbor," August 1938. SHL.

12. Collier, 99.

13. Ibid., 100.

14. Dorr, Book II, 76.

15. John D. Rockefeller, Jr., Letter to the editor, *Bar Harbor Times,* 5/1/41. RAC.

16. Raymond B. Fosdick, *John D. Rockefeller, Jr., A Portrait* (New York: Harper & Brothers, 1956), 140.

17. Ibid., 142.

18. George Dorr, Letter to JDR Jr., 9/11/14. RAC.

19. JDR Jr., Letter to George Dorr, 2/8/18. RAC.

20. Fosdick, 304.

Chapter 3. The Road Work Begins

1. Raymond B. Fosdick, *John D. Rockefeller, Jr., A Portrait* (New York: Harper & Brothers, 1956), 129.

2. Fosdick, 302.

3. Laurance S. Rockefeller, Conversation with author, 3/24/88.

4. Dana Creel, Conversation with author, 2/21/88.

5. John D. Rockefeller, Jr., Letter to Arno B. Cammerer, 12/15/27. RAC.

6. Charles P. Simpson, Conversation with author, 7/13/89.

7. George Dorr, Letter to JDR Jr., 2/19/15. RAC.

8. Ibid.

9. Charles W. Eliot, Letter to JDR Jr., 9/13/19. RAC.

10. Laurance S. Rockefeller, Conversation with author.

11. Freeman Tilden, "Friend of Our Heritage," unpublished manuscript, 11. RAC.

12. Ibid., 10.

13. Charles W. Eliot, Letter to JDR Jr., 2/25/15. RAC.

14. Charles W. Eliot, Letter to JDR Jr., 8/30/16. RAC.

15. Charles W. Eliot, Letter to JDR Jr., 9/30/16. RAC.

16. Charles P. Simpson II, Conversation with author.

17. Ibid.

18. Irene Hill Marinke, Conversation with author, July 1989.

19. JDR Jr., Letter to George Dorr, 2/8/18. RAC.

20. JDR Jr., Letter to Horace M. Albright, 3/14/35. Acadia National Park Archives.

21. George Dorr, Letter to JDR Jr., 2/12/18. RAC.

22. JDR Jr., Letter to George Dorr, 3/18/18. RAC.

Chapter 4. Perseverance Amid Controversy

1. George Wharton Pepper, Letter to JDR Jr., 8/15/20. RAC.

2. John D. Rockefeller, Jr., Letter to George Wharton Pepper, 8/20/20. RAC.

3. JDR Jr., Letter to Lincoln Cromwell, 9/1/20, quoted in *Bar Harbor Times*, 9/8/20. RAC.

4. George Wharton Pepper, Letter to JDR Jr., 9/2/20. RAC.

5. *Bar Harbor Times*, 9/8/20. RAC.

6. George Dorr, Letter to Lincoln Cromwell, 9/1/20. RAC.

7. Petitions from citizens re Amphitheatre Road, September 1920. RAC.

8. *Bar Harbor Times,* 9/8/20. RAC.

9. JDR Jr., Letter to George Wharton Pepper, 9/16/20. RAC.

10. JDR Jr., Letter to Lincoln Cromwell, 9/1/20. RAC.

11. JDR Jr., Letter to F.H. Macomber, 9/8/20. RAC.

12. JDR Jr., Letter to George Dorr, 7/12/22. RAC.

13. George Dorr, Letter to JDR Jr., 10/3/22. RAC.

14. JDR Jr., Letter to George Dorr, 10/6/22. RAC

15. JDR Jr., Letter to A.E. Clement, 5/6/26. RAC.

16. Reports of Arno B. Cammerer to Stephen P. Mather, Director, National Park Service, June 1922, quoted in *Bar Harbor Times*, 3/26/24. Bar Harbor Historical Society.

17. JDR Jr., Letter to George Wharton Pepper, 9/16/20. RAC.

18. Herbert Gleason, in *Boston Evening Transcript*, 8/9/24. RAC.

19. Conversation with Kenneth Chorley (interviewer unidentified), 10/26/54. RAC.

20. Freeman Tilden, "Friend of Our Heritage," unpublished manuscript, Chapter 4, 1–2. RAC.

21. Paul D. Simpson, Letter to JDR Jr., 3/18/24. Personal collection of Charles P. Simpson, Seal Harbor, Maine.

22. JDR Jr., Letter to George Dorr, 3/24/24. RAC.

23. Hubert Work, Letter to George Dorr, 7/25/24. Acadia National Park.

24. JDR Jr., Letter to Paul D. Simpson, 12/22/26. Personal collection of Charles P. Simpson II, Seal Harbor, Maine.

25. Bishop William Lawrence, Committee report from *The Future of Mount Desert Island,* by Charles W. Eliot 2nd, landscape architect, Bar Harbor Village Improvement Association, 1928.

26. JDR Jr., Letter to Arno B. Cammerer, 9/3/26. RAC.

27. Arno B. Cammerer, Letter to JDR Jr., 9/7/26. RAC.

28. Charles W. Eliot 2nd, *The Future of Mount Desert Island: A Report to the Planning Committee, Bar Harbor Village Improvement Association* (1928), 25–26.

29. JDR Jr., Letter to Paul D. Simpson, 3/21/31. Personal collection of Charles P. Simpson, Seal Harbor, Maine.

30. *Bar Harbor Times,* 12/3/30.

31. JDR Jr., Letter to Arno B. Cammerer, 9/24/32. RAC.

32. JDR Jr., Letter to Secretary of the Interior Ray Lyman Wilbur, 8/16/32. RAC.

33. Raymond B. Fosdick, Interview with JDR Jr., 9/29/53. RAC.

Chapter 5. Practical Matters

1. John D. Rockefeller, Jr., Letter to A.E. Clement, 12/12/18. RAC.

2. JDR Jr., Letter to Paul D. Simpson, 1/25/18. RAC.

3. *The Carriage Roads at Acadia National Park: Resource Study* (draft), June 1988, prepared by Rieley & Associates for the National Park Service. NPS.

4. JDR Jr., Road specifications, sent to A.E. Clement, 9/24/18. RAC.

5. JDR Jr., Letter to A.E. Clement, 12/17/18. RAC.

6. David Rockefeller, Conversation with author, 8/19/87.

7. JDR Jr., Letter to George Dorr, 8/21/35. RAC.

8. JDR Jr., Road specifications, 9/24/18. RAC.

9. George Dorr, "Specifications for a Horse Road on Mount Desert Island," enclosure in letter to A.E. Clement, 10/9/22. RAC.

10. Ibid.

11. JDR Jr., Letter to Chauncey D. Joy, 10/21/26. RAC.

12. Robert Pyle, Conversation with author, 7/19/89.

13. Victor J. Layton, "Mt. Desert Island's Granite Heritage," *Down East* 28 (June 1982), 78.

14. JDR Jr., Letter to Charles S. Simpson, 3/29/19. RAC.

15. JDR Jr., Letter to Paul D. Simpson, 5/29/23. RAC.

16. JDR Jr., Letter to Chauncey D. Joy, 7/17/25. RAC.

17. Paul D. Simpson, Letter to JDR Jr., 1/19/31. Personal collection of Charles P. Simpson II, Seal Harbor, Maine.

18. JDR Jr., Letter to Paul D. Simpson, 1/31/31. Acadia National Park Archives.

19. Layton, p. 76.

20. Grosvenor Atterbury, "Notes on the Architectural and Other Esthetic Problems Involved in the Development of Our National Parks," 1929. Personal collection of Marion Schenk, Studio City, California.

21. Charles E. Peterson, Memorandum to director of National Park Service, 10/27/31. RAC.

22. JDR Jr., Letter to Beatrix Farrand, 7/21/31. RAC.

23. JDR Jr., Letter to Beatrix Farrand, 5/16/29. RAC.

24. Beatrix Farrand, Letter to JDR Jr., 5/22/29. RAC.

25. JDR Jr., Letter to Beatrix Farrand, 7/31/31. RAC.

26. JDR Jr., Letter to Horace M. Albright, 11/11/24. RAC.

27. Beatrix Farrand, Rockefeller Road Notes, 10/2/29. RAC.

28. Ibid.

29. Beatrix Farrand, Letter to JDR Jr., 6/3/32. RAC.

30. Farrand, Road Notes, 11/4/30. RAC.

31. JDR Jr., Letter to Beatrix Farrand, 5/26/32. RAC.

32. Beatrix Farrand, Letter to JDR Jr., 6/3/32. RAC.

33. Farrand, Road Notes, 11/4/30. RAC.

34. Ibid., 10/13/32. RAC.

35. Beatrix Farrand, Letter to JDR Jr., 3/29/30. RAC.

36. Farrand, Road Notes, 10/2/29. RAC.

37. JDR Jr., Letter to Beatrix Farrand, 7/31/31. RAC.

38. Beatrix Farrand, Letter to JDR Jr., 5/10/32. RAC.

39. Beatrix Farrand, Letter to JDR Jr., 5/17/32. RAC.

Epilogue

1. Edward R. Finch, Letter to JDR Jr., 7/9/37. RAC.

2. Brigadier General Hayes Kroner, Letter to JDR Jr., 8/29/48. RAC.

Bibliography

Note: The following abbreviations have been used throughout this bibliography: RAC—Rockefeller Archive Center, Tarrytown, New York; SHL—Seal Harbor Library, Mount Desert Island, Maine; NPS—National Park Service, Washington, D.C.

Abrell, Diana F. *A Guide to the Carriage Roads In & Near Acadia National Park.* Camden, Maine: Down East Books, 1985.

Albright, Horace M., as told to Robert Cahn. *The Birth of the National Park Service: The Founding Years 1913–33.* Salt Lake City: Howe Brothers, 1985.

————. Papers. Personal collection of Marion Schenk, Studio City, California.

Allen, Albert. Conversation with author. Seal Harbor, Maine, July 1987.

Atterbury, Grosvenor. "Notes on the Architectural and Other Esthetic Problems Involved in the Development of Our Great National Parks." Unpublished, August/September 1929.

Bar Harbor Times, Bar Harbor, Maine, 1920s, 1930s.

Breeze, Benjamin L. "A Land Status Study of Acadia National Park, Mount Desert Island, Maine," August 20, 1942 (NPS files).

Burgess, Larry E. *Mohonk: Its People and Spirit.* Mohonk, New York: Mohonk Mountain House, 1980.

Butcher, Pam, and Russell D. Butcher. "Carriage Roads and Bridges of Acadia National Park." *Down East,* August 1972, 52–87.

Butcher, Russell D. "The Jordan Pond House," *Down East,* July 1970, 52–116.

Carter, Lydia B. "Early History of Seal Harbor," January 1959 (SHL).

Chorley, Kenneth. Conversation with unidentified interviewer, October 26, 1954 (RAC).

Collier, Clare. Conversation with author. Tarrytown, New York, July 1987.

Collier, Sargent F. *Mt. Desert Island and Acadia National Park: An Informal History.* Camden, Maine: Down East Books, 1978.

————. *The Triumph of George B. Dorr.* Private printing, 1964.

Creel, Dana. Conversation with author, February 21, 1988.

Dane, Edward S., "Recollections." Unpublished, August 1931 (SHL).

Dorr, George B. *Acadia National Park: Its Origins and Background.* Bangor, Maine: Burr Printing Company, 1942.

————. *Acadia National Park: Its Growth and Development.* Bangor, Maine: Burr Printing Company, 1948.

————. *The Story of Acadia National Park.* Two books in one. Bar Harbor, Maine: Acadia Publishing Co., 1942.

Downing, Andrew Jackson. *A Treatise on the Theory and Practice of Landscape*

Gardening Adapted to North America. New York: Riker, Thorne & Co., 1854 edition.

Eliot, Charles W., 2nd. *The Future of Mount Desert Island: A Report to the Planning Committee, Bar Harbor Village Improvement Association,* 1928.

Eliot, Charles W. *The Right Development of Mount Desert.* Private printing, 1904 (Northeast Harbor Library).

Fosdick, Raymond B. *John D. Rockefeller, Jr., A Portrait.* New York: Harper & Brothers, 1956.

Glacken, Clarence. *Traces on the Rhodian Shore.* Los Angeles: UCLA Press, 1967.

Goulder, Grace. *John D. Rockefeller—The Cleveland Years.* Cleveland: The Western Reserve Historical Society, 1972.

Hale, Richard Walden, Jr. *The Story of Bar Harbor.* New York: Ives Washburn Inc., 1949.

Hamilton, Nelson. Conversation with author. Town Hill, Maine, July 1987.

Harr, John Ensor, and Peter J. Johnson. *The Rockefeller Century.* New York: Charles Scribner's Sons, 1988.

Howat, John K. *The Hudson River and Its Painters.* New York: American Legacy Press, 1983.

Hubbard, Henry Vincent, and Theodora Kimball. *An Introduction to the Study of Landscape Design.* New York: Macmillan, 1927.

Ingliss, William O. "In Happiness & In Sorrow." Unpublished, p. 667, (RAC).

Irving, Washington. *The Sketch Book of Geoffrey Crayon, Gent.* Philadelphia: J.B. Lippincott, 1873.

"John D. Rockefeller, Junior, Lover of Order and Excellence," *Landscape Architecture* 28, no. 3 (April 1938): 136–143.

Journal of Friends of Acadia, vol. 1, no. 1. Bar Harbor, Maine, 1987.

Layton, Victor J. "Mt. Desert Island's Granite Heritage." *Down East,* June 1982, 74–78.

Maine Geological Survey, Department of Conservtion. *The Geology of Mount Desert Island.* Augusta: Maine Geological Survey, 1988.

Mancinelli, Isabel, LA. Conversation with author. Bar Harbor, Maine, July 1987.

Morison, Samuel Eliot. *The Story of Mount Desert Island.* Boston: Little, Brown, 1960.

Nash, Roderick. *Wilderness and the American Mind.* New Haven: Yale University Press, 1982.

National Park Service. *Rules and Regulations: Lafayette National Park.* Washington, D.C.: Government Printing Office, 1921.

Newhall, Nancy. *A Contribution to the Heritage of Every American—The Conservation Activities of John D. Rockefeller, Jr.* New York: Alfred A. Knopf, 1959.

Newton, Norman T. *Design on the Land—The Development of Landscape Architecture.* Cambridge: Harvard University Press, 1971.

Olmsted, Frederick L., Jr., and Theodora Kimball, eds. *Frederick Law Olmsted—Landscape Architect 1822–1903.* New York: Benjamin Blom, Inc. 1970.

"150th Anniversary of the Founding of Seal Harbor in 1809," *Bar Harbor Times,* August 20, 1959.

Pyle, Tom. *Pocantico: Fifty Years on the Rockefeller Domain.* New York: Duell, Sloan and Pearce, 1964.

Pyle, Robert. Conversation with author. July 1989.

Rieley, William D., and Roxanne S. Brouse. *The Carriage Roads at Acadia National Park: Resource Study.* Draft report prepared for the National Park Service. Charlottesville, Virginia: Rieley and Associates, Landscape Architects, June 1988 (NPS).

———. *Historic Resource Study for the Carriage Road System, Acadia National Park, Mount Desert Island, Maine.* Final report prepared for the National Park Service. Charlottesville, Virginia: Rieley and Associates, Landscape Architects, May 1989 (NPS).

Rockefeller, David. Conversation with author. Tarrytown, New York, August 1987.

Rockefeller, John D. *Random Reminiscences of Men and Events.* Edited by Laurance S. Rockefeller. Tarrytown, New York: Sleepy Hollow Press, 1984.

Rockefeller, John D., Jr. Correspondence. Acadia National Park Archives, Bar Harbor, Maine.

———. Papers, 1900–1935 (RAC).

Rockefeller, Laurance S. Conversation with author. New York City, July 1987.

Rockefeller, Mary C. Conversation with author. Northeast Harbor, Maine, July 1987.

Simpson, Charles P. Conversation with author, July 13, 1989.

Simpson, Paul D. Papers. Personal Collection of Charles P. Simpson, Seal Harbor, Maine.

Stebbins, George L. "Random Notes on the Early History and Development as a Summer Resort of Mount Desert Island and particularly Seal Harbor." Unpublished, August 1938 (SHL).

Taylor, A.D. *Forest Hill Park—A Report on the Proposed Landscape Development.* Cleveland: Caxton Co., 1938.

Tilden, Freeman, "Friend of Our Heritage." Unpublished (RAC).

Tilden, Freeman. *The National Parks.* New York: Alfred A. Knopf, 1986.

Tucker, William. "Environmentalism and the Leisure Class." *Harper's,* December 1977: 49–80.

Winter, Lois. Conversation with author. Bar Harbor, Maine, July 1987.

Written in the Rocks. Acadia National Park brochure, n.d.

Wylock, Ray. Conversation with author. Tarrytown, New York, July 1987.

Index